Yayoi Kusama

Infinity M

– Phalli's

Jo Applin

One Work Series Editor
Mark Lewis

Afterall Books Editorial Directors
Charles Esche and Mark Lewis

Editor
Pablo Lafuente

Managing Editor
Gaia Alessi

Associate Editor
Caroline Woodley

Editorial Assistant
Louise O'Hare

Copy Editor
Deirdre O'Dwyer

Other titles in the *One Work* series:

Bas Jan Ader: In Search of the Miraculous
by Jan Verwoert

Hollis Frampton: (nostalgia)
by Rachel Moore

Ilya Kabakov: The Man Who Flew into Space from his Apartment
by Boris Groys

Richard Prince: Untitled (couple)
by Michael Newman

Joan Jonas: I Want to Live in the Country (And Other Romances)
by Susan Morgan

Mary Heilmann: Save the Last Dance for Me
by Terry R. Myers

Marc Camille Chaimowicz: Celebration? Realife
by Tom Holert

Yvonne Rainer: The Mind is a Muscle
by Catherine Wood

Fischli and Weiss: The Way Things Go
by Jeremy Millar

Andy Warhol: Blow Job
by Peter Gidal

Alighiero e Boetti: Mappa
by Luca Cerizza

Chris Marker: La Jetée
by Janet Harbord

Hanne Darboven: Cultural History 1880–1983
by Dan Adler

Michael Snow: Wavelength
by Elizabeth Legge

Sarah Lucas: Au Naturel
by Amna Malik

Richard Long: A Line Made by Walking
by Dieter Roelstraete

Marcel Duchamp: Étant donnés
by Julian Jason Haladyn

General Idea: Imagevirus
by Gregg Bordowitz

Dara Birnbaum: Technology/Transformation: Wonder Woman
by T.J. Demos

Gordon Matta-Clark: Conical Intersect
by Bruce Jenkins

Jeff Wall: Picture for Women
by David Campany

Jeff Koons: One Ball Total Equilibrium Tank
by Michael Archer

Richard Hamilton: Swingeing London 67 (f)
by Andrew Wilson

Martha Rosler: The Bowery in two inadequate descriptive systems
by Steve Edwards

Dan Graham: Rock My Religion
by Kodwo Eshun

Michael Asher: Kunsthalle Bern, 1992
by Anne Rorimer

One Work is a unique series of books published by Afterall, based at Central Saint Martins College of Art and Design in London. Each book presents a single work of art considered in detail by a single author. The focus of the series is on contemporary art and its aim is to provoke debate about significant moments in art's recent development.

Over the course of more than one hundred books, important works will be presented in a meticulous and generous manner by writers who believe passionately in the originality and significance of the works about which they have chosen to write. Each book contains a comprehensive and detailed formal description of the work, followed by a critical mapping of the aesthetic and cultural context in which it was made and has gone on to shape. The changing presentation and reception of the work throughout its existence is also discussed, and each writer stakes a claim on the influence 'their' work has on the making and understanding of other works of art.

The books insist that a single contemporary work of art (in all of its different manifestations), through a unique and radical aesthetic articulation or invention, can affect our understanding of art in general. More than that, these books suggest that a single work of art can literally transform, however modestly, the way we look at and understand the world. In this sense the *One Work* series, while by no means exhaustive, will eventually become a veritable library of works of art that have made a difference.

First published in 2012
by Afterall Books

Afterall
Central Saint Martins
College of Art and Design,
University of the Arts London
Granary Building
1 Granary Square
London N1C 4AA
www.afterall.org

ISBN Paperback: 978-1-84638-091-4
ISBN Cloth: 978-1-84638-090-7

Distribution by The MIT Press,
Cambridge, Massachusetts and London
www.mitpress.mit.edu

Art Direction and Typeface Design
A2/SW/HK

Printed and bound by
Die Keure, Belgium

The *One Work* series is printed
on FSC-certified papers

Supported using public funding by
ARTS COUNCIL
ENGLAND

Yayoi Kusama

Infinity Mirror Room – Phalli's Field

Jo Applin

A number of friends and colleagues offered invaluable advice and support during the writing of this book, and I would like in the first instance to thank them. This book has benefited enormously from the work of other Kusama scholars, and my debt to their scholarship is evident in the following pages. In particular, many thanks are due to Midori Yamamura, who has been incredibly generous in her support of my work on Yayoi Kusama, and shared her archival findings on the artist with me. I am grateful for the period of leave funded by the University of York that enabled me to complete this manuscript. A special and heartfelt thank you to Yayoi Kusama, and to the staff at her studio for all their help and kind support of this project, and also to Victoria Miro gallery in London. The editors would also like to thank Yayoi Kusama and her studio for their invaluable help with images and information.

Jo Applin is Lecturer in the History of Art Department at the University of York. She has written widely on modern and contemporary art in journals including *Artforum*, *Art History*, *Art Journal*, *parallax*, *Oxford Art Journal* and *Tate Papers*. She has recently published essays on Lee Lozano (Moderna Museet, 2010) and Yayoi Kusama (Tate, 2012) and her book *Eccentric Objects: Rethinking Sculpture in 1960s America* was published in 2012 by Yale University Press.

For RT

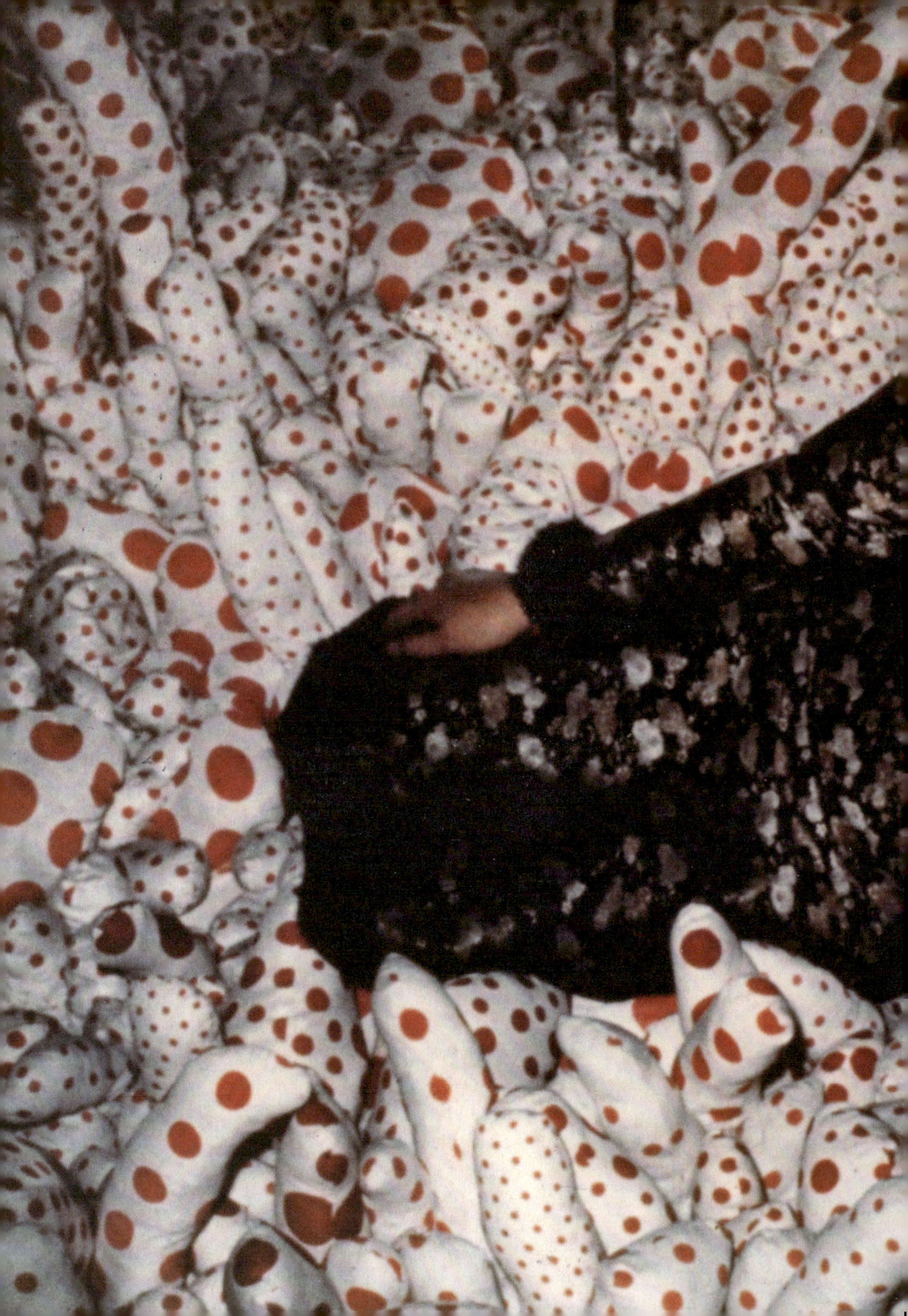

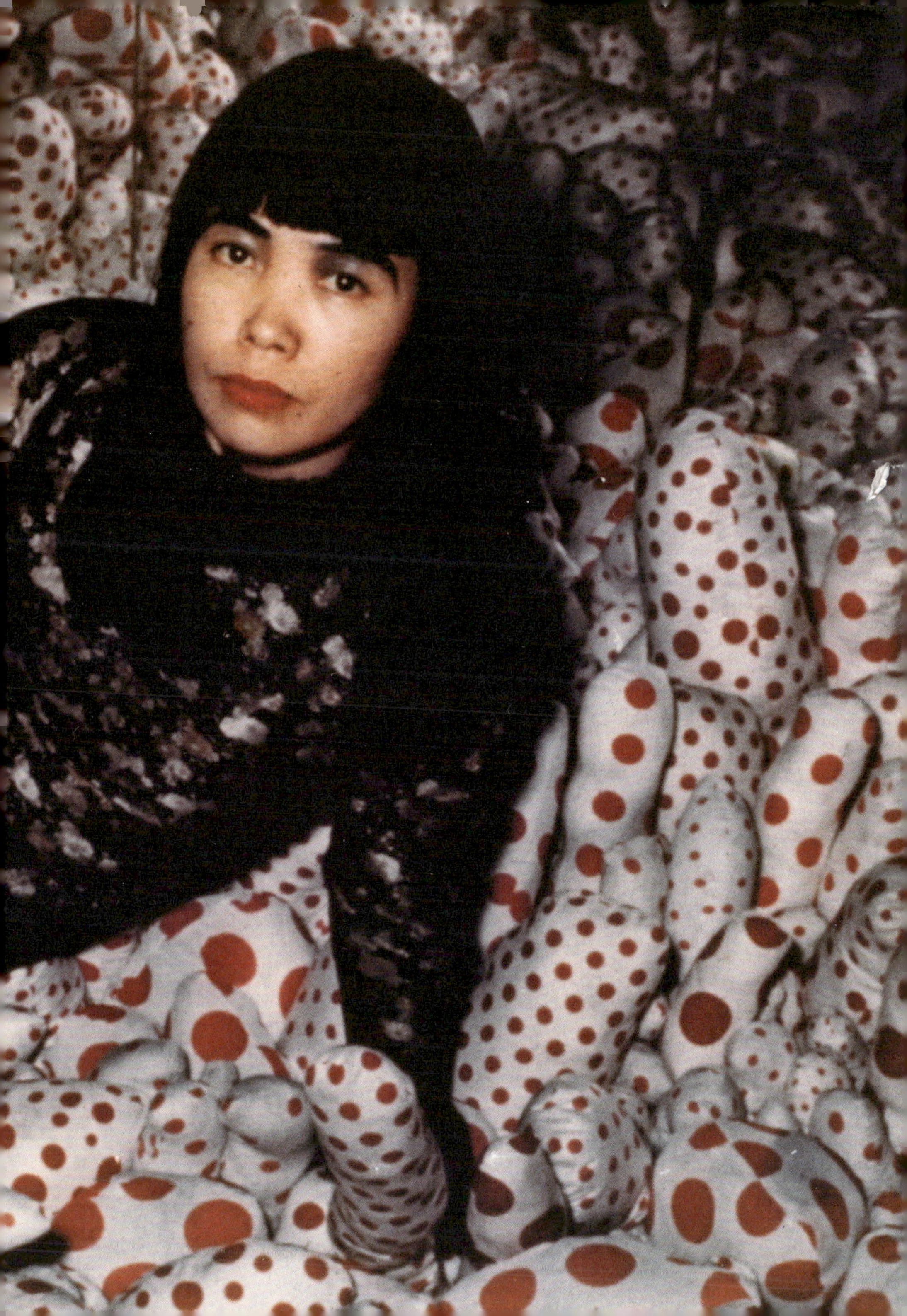

cover and previous pages

Yayoi Kusama,
Infinity Mirror Room — Phalli's Field, 1965,
sewn stuffed fabric, mirrors,
455 × 455 × 250cm,
installation view, Kusama lying on the floor, 'Floor Show', Richard Castellane Gallery, New York, 1965

Contents

Infinity Mirror Room – Phalli's Field

> *This area of playing is not inner psychic reality. It is outside the individual, but it is not the external world.*
> — D.W. Winnicott[1]

Infinity Mirror Room — Phalli's Field, a mixed-media room-sized installation by the Japanese artist Yayoi Kusama, was first exhibitied in 1965. It was shown as part of Kusama's solo exhibition 'Floor Show', held at the Richard Castellane Gallery in New York, just seven years after she had arrived in the city (fig.1—5).[2] The mirrored room, specially constructed for the show, measured just over two and a half metres high, with a floor surface of 25 square metres. It was situated in the first room of the gallery, a room within a room, which lent the work an added sense of enclosure and containment. The four walls of *Infinity Mirror Room — Phalli's Field* were lined with mirrored panels from top to bottom, reflecting the viewer's image endlessly back and forth. Save for a narrow pathway, the floor of the room was covered with a carpet of several hundred soft fabric protuberances that Kusama had made by stitching together sections of polka dot-printed cotton fabric. Each of the white and red sacs was stuffed tightly with wadding, packed to stand taut and upright, arranged in crowded and haphazard clusters on rectangular sheets of plywood. Together they formed what Kusama has described as a 'sublime, miraculous field of phalluses'.[3] Within their limited remit, however, there were considerable differences. Kusama used several different kinds of red polka dot fabric to make the tubers, from big fat spots to uniform rows of small dots. This was no perfect serial arrangement of identical units; rather, the 'phallic field' figured as a tumbling riot of tumescent forms, ranging from the short and dumpy to the long and spindly, providing an inviting and surprisingly springy three-dimensional surface.

The protuberances — so 'bodily' and yet so clearly *not* of the body — were witty, eccentric forms, situated somewhere between erotic part-objects[4] and funny playthings, as Kusama would demonstrate in the photographs she took of her own body placed inside the room, against the soft forms (fig.1—4 and 7). Kusama later recalled how she had imagined people 'wandering into this infinite wonderland, where a grandiose aggregation of human sexual symbols had been transformed into a humorous, polka-dotted field'.[5] On entering the room, visitors would 'walk barefoot through the phallus meadow, becoming one with the work and experiencing their own figures and movements as part of the sculpture'.[6]

Visitors entered *Infinity Mirror Room — Phalli's Field* through a doorway. Once inside, they saw themselves mirrored against the red and white background of fabric bulges, with which they would, in Kusama's words, 'become one'. The endless repetition of visitors' bodies cast each as an object among many others — as animate, bodily counterparts to their inanimate spotty doubles. 'Soft sculpture is alive', Kusama announced in 1969, drawing attention to these anthropomorphic qualities.[7] One black-and-white photograph taken during the opening of the exhibition depicts a small dog sitting calmly in the soft field (fig.5). The animal is hard to see in the photograph, as its spotty fur coat is camouflaged amongst the polka dots — its body almost hidden by the squashy phallic tubers. In this photograph, foreground and background blur into a flat, continuous spotted surface. Self and other, inside and outside, animate and inanimate — familiar binaries around which social, physical and psychological relationships are typically organised — are momentarily destabilised in this image. As Alexandra Munroe has pointed out, 'The cheery look of the scene is deceptive and ironic', as Kusama 'actualises' for the viewer a series of dizzying, hallucinatory encounters.[8] While only alluded to playfully in this photograph, the psychological effects of such a loss of one's sense of self is a theme Kusama has returned to time and again in her work — a diverse corpus that encompasses her *Infinity Net* paintings (fig.8 and 9), in which large canvases are covered in immersive patterns of nets and dots; phallic-studded sculptural objects; disorienting room environments; and public 'happenings' or performances. *Infinity Mirror Room — Phalli's Field* incorporates Kusama's key formal motifs, from the stuffed fabric phallic tubers to the polka dots spotting every available surface and object, and her striking use of mirrors to produce the unsettling interior *mise en abyme* that would become her trademark.[9]

With *Infinity Mirror Room — Phalli's Field*, Kusama set out to 'create a "Kusama World" which no one has ever done or trodden into'.[10] The room produces phenomenological and psychological uncertainty in participants, who are equipped with neither script nor strategy. The work is at once an invitation and a series of unanswered questions. It places demands on its visitor, although quite how she is expected to behave within its mirrored walls is not clear — is it supposed to be entered alone or with other people? Is it an environment in which the subject is trapped or set free, accommodated or made alien? Is this an inviting, playful 'open work', in which the spectator is a necessary and welcome participant, or is this an ominous and destabilising environment marked by dislocation and discomfort, in which she is set adrift, lost in 'Kusama World'?[11]

This psychogically charged mode of encounter is a theme that has dominated Kusama's work to date. Endlessly reflected, the visitor to *Infinity Mirror Room — Phalli's Field* experiences herself as though trapped within a kaleidoscopic regime that serves to pull the rug from under her feet — questions of what is real and what is not, of 'who am I?' and 'where am I?' are playfully yet powerfully posed. With this work, Kusama sought to capture something of the very real and debilitating periods of psychological breakdown she has experienced since childhood.[12]

Kusama has repeatedly described how she suffers from episodes of extreme hallucinosis, disassociation disorder and intense anxiety.[13] When describing such distressing psychological episodes, she has recounted how she feels her bodily boundaries breaking down, as she experiences herself absorbed by, or dissolved, within her environment. During these encounters Kusama feels herself flattening out and blurring into one continuous surface in which she, through a form of psychic camouflage, experiences herself as lost to her environment. *Infinity Mirror Room — Phalli's Field* provides a visual analogue for those instances of psychological disorder, in which Kusama finds her body submerged within an infinite sea of polka dots. In relation to this, she has described the process of making art as a form of self-therapy:[14]

> *I often suffered episodes of severe neurosis. I would cover a canvas with nets, then continue painting them on the table, on the floor and finally on my own body. As I repeated this process over and over again, the nets began to expand to infinity. I forgot about myself as they enveloped me, clinging to my arms and legs and clothes and filling the entire room.*[15]

Kusama has recalled that when she is overcome by her obsessional neuroses, she feels 'tormented by a thin, silk-like curtain of indeterminate grey ... between me and my surroundings'.[16] In recounting one particularly vivid hallucination, she writes: 'I woke one morning to find the nets I had painted the previous day stuck to the windows. Marvelling at this, I went to touch them, and they crawled on and into the skin of my hands. My heart began racing.'[17]

Infinity Mirror Room — Phalli's Field offers a three-dimensional version of Kusama's earlier *Infinity Net* paintings, which she began to make in 1958. The hallucinatory aspect of the abstract nets in the paintings is rendered literal and material in the hundreds of red spotted forms that occupy the same space as the visitors. Surrealist writer Roger Caillois described the psychological and physiological process of mimetic blurring with one's environment in his essay 'Mimicry and Legendary Psychasthenia' (1935), in which he offered as a case study of the role of camouflage in the animal world. Psychasthenia describes an anxious-obsessive compulsive condition, which Caillois compared to the way in which certain animals and insects merge into their surroundings to become 'invisible' at the first sign of danger — a condition that describes, too, Kusama's experience of 'self-obliteration'.[18]

To visualise the kind of psychologically charged interior space that Kusama produced, *Infinity Mirror Room — Phalli's Field* might be considered alongside the noteworthy short story 'The Yellow Wallpaper' (1892) by the US novelist and early champion of women's rights Charlotte Perkins Gilman.[19] The narrator of 'The Yellow Wallpaper' is a young woman who has been confined to her bed, ostensibly to recover from a nervous condition. When alone, she hallucinates that the patterned wallpaper covering the walls of her room is coming to life. Simultaneously terrified and fascinated, the woman finds herself obsessed by the immersive, mobile patterns:

> *It is dull enough to confuse the eye in following, pronounced enough to constantly irritate and provoke study, and when you follow the lame uncertain curves for a little distance they suddenly commit suicide — plunge off at outrageous angles, destroy themselves in unheard of contradictions.*[20]

Staring at the yellow wallpaper from her bed, she comes to believe that there is another woman trapped behind it, pressing the patterned paper away from the wall and into the room's interior space. By the story's final pages, the young narrator, caught up in a psychasthenic nightmare, has left the safety of her bed to frantically tear at the paper lining the room, only to find that it 'sticks horribly' as its pattern of 'bulbous eyes and waddling fungus growths' begins to envelop her body.[21] By the end, the 'she' designating the woman behind the wallpaper and the 'I' of the narrator become confused. As the narrator becomes the woman trapped behind the wallpaper, dissolving into its fibrous weft, the wallpaper and her body become one another in a movement that she experiences as both ecstatic and obliterating. The young woman finally breaks free from her environment — by succumbing to it and to the mental illness it allegorises — and triumphantly declares to her husband 'I've got out at last... And I've pulled off most of the paper, so you can't put me back!'[22] Gilman's account — marked as it is by fear, depression and 'self-obliteration' — offers a vivid version of the making and viewing of Kusama's *Infinity Net* paintings, as well as the crammed and riotous accretion of phallic spotted knobs that similarly 'confuse the eye' in *Infinity Mirror Room — Phalli's Field.*

Kusama was temporarily hospitalised several times in the 1960s, while living in New York. She has described these episodes of psychological disorder, when she feels herself scatter into her environment, as the sensation of 'dissolution and accumulation. Proliferation and fragmentation. The feeling of myself obliterating.'[23] In what follows, I want to attend to Kusama's own strategic framing of her condition, the *use* to which Kusama puts that vocabulary of 'dissolution' and 'proliferation'. She offers a language of obliteration but also of freedom that provides the means through which she reframes the personal as the political — just as Gilman did in her narrative of the young female protagonist who desired personal freedom above all else. Gilman's text is an early feminist treatise, offering a powerful image of a young woman whose freedom is attained by extraordinary, damaging and, crucially, fantastical means — the impossibility of that final 'escape' as she frees herself from her paper binding to fly out of the room, to be free. The confined interior space of *Infinity Mirror Room — Phalli's Field* embodies one way in which subjects experience and encounter both the artwork and the world. In so doing, Kusama's interior, like Gilman's, offers a surprising and prescient framework for how we might think about each.

Kusama, however, is no outspoken feminist. Since the 1960s she has resisted affiliation with the women's movement and with the work of other female artists. This is not to say that her work does not provide a powerful model for thinking through questions of subjectivity. Despite Kusama's ongoing reticence to ally herself with feminist artists, made explicit in a number of one-page 'press releases' that she produced periodically during the 1960s, she has often hailed the polka dot as a symbol of femininity, reproduction and nature.[24] It is, however, fear of sex that has frequently been offered as an explanation for the endless repetition of the phallic form across her work. She folds these forms into a narrative often repeated to interviewers and in her own writings, about transforming or sublating her fears into something unthreatening, something playful or 'funny':

> *By continuously reproducing the forms of things that terrify me, I am able to suppress the fear. I make a pile of soft sculpture penises and lie down among them. That turns the frightening thing into something funny, something amusing.*[25]

In keeping with the rhetorical bombast of her press releases, Kusama has explained her use of polka dots more broadly as an allegory of the human condition. For Kusama, the polka dot symbolised togetherness and unity: 'Polka dots must always multiply to infinity. Our earth is only one polka dot among millions of others. When Kusama paints your body with polka dots you become part of the unity of the universe.'[26] For Kusama, the polka dot is a formal means of flattening out difference and uniting diverse bodies, objects and surfaces — a mode of being together that, as we shall see, has the potential to be both utopian and dystopian, unifying and destabilising, political and playful. Kusama's most pronounced articulation of that ambiguity is figured in *Infinity Mirror Room — Phalli's Field*. This one work by Kusama offers a strikingly original model for thinking about the work of art as an expanded and participatory environment. Prior to the recent 'participatory turn' in contemporary art, in which questions of relationality have come to the fore, Kusama turned her interior world into a shared and public one — open to all who wished to enter into it as willing visitors (for isn't 'participation' simply another word for what *all* works of art invite their visitors to do?)[27] By doing this, Kusama sought to make the personal political, and her private, psychological world a social, shared one that offered visitors (whether 'barefoot' or not) experiences that veered between pleasure and paranoia, fear and bliss, self-knowledge and self-obliteration.

Psychotic Art

Walking into the second room of Kusama's 'Floor Show' exhibition at Richard Castellane Gallery, after having passed through *Infinity Mirror Room — Phalli's Field*, visitors found themselves embroiled in a scenario in which the humdrum environment of the domestic sphere was revealed as psychosexual drama. The room was filled with *Accumulation* sculptures, which Kusama had first begun to make in 1962. Ordinary, everyday items covered with stuffed fabric phalli, these sculptures have been described as revelling in an 'everyday domesticity gone awry'.[28] Hundreds of phallic forms packed with wadding (often pulled from the inside of mattresses) engulfed every available surface of the shoes, ironing boards, ladders and dustpans on display. They were variously made from multicoloured polka dot-patterned fabrics, or painted monochromatically white, silver or gold. When attached to once-familiar household items, the 'accumulations' (or 'aggregations', as she also called the phalli-covered objects) register less as 'field' and more as fungal overgrowths (fig.12). Other items Kusama included in the second room of 'Floor Show' were her first *Accumulation* pieces of furniture from 1962: the white armchair *Accumulation 1* and sofa *Accumulation 2* (fig.10). In 1964 Kusama began to exhibit the studded domestic items in a series of dizzying and crammed domestic tableaux, under the title *Driving Image*. By colonising the space and surface of the room with clusters of phallic tubers, Kusama was able to continue the lateral spread of the phallic carpet from the overstuffed interior of *Infinity Mirror Room — Phalli's Field*, producing an installation that offered precisely that mix of playful chaos and psychosexual drama that was becoming a defining theme of her artistic output.

Kusama's humorously absurd staging of the familiar as a sexual fetish object was emphasised in two works included in 'Floor Show': *Travelling Life* (1964) and *Baby Carriage* (1964/66). *Travelling Life* features three pairs of phallus-covered high-heeled shoes that adorn the steps of a splayed-open ladder (rendering both the shoes and the ladder unusable), while *Baby Carriage* employs a pram as a receptacle not for a small infant but for a bundle of phallic objects. These two works share much with Surrealist precursors, such as Meret Oppenheim's *Object* (1936),[29] a cup, saucer and spoon lined in Chinese gazelle fur, and Man Ray's *Cadeau* (*Gift*, 1921), a tack-studded metal iron; both were similarly wrenched from the utilitarian sphere of the domestic to one of fantasy and violence, of play, touch and eroticism. Starting in 1962, Kusama grouped her *Accumulation* sculptures into categories, including *Sex-Obsession*, *Food-Obsession* and *Compulsion Furniture*. Together these objects appear as harbingers of a consumerist fantasy turned nightmare, a theme that Kusama continued to pursue. The sculptures and mannequins she would soon begin to cover with dried pasta, further demonstrated the extent to which we as subjects are at the mercy of the objects we consume, as they in turn consume us.

Alongside the fetish-studded ladder, baby carriage, sofa and other repurposed objects strewn about the room, Kusama included her recent large-scale blood-red sculpture *My Flower Bed* (1962), an enormous drooping plant-like object that she made from hundreds of white cotton workman's gloves that her father had mailed to her from Japan. Kusama dip-dyed the knitted gloves red, stuffed and clumped them together as abject, fanned-out 'leaves', sprouting from red-stained bases made from reclaimed mattress springs.[30] Like the ladder, shoes, armchair and sofa, *My Flower Bed* would have registered as an extension of *Infinity Mirror Room — Phalli's Field* — as an alien life form echoing the spotted forms inside the adjacent mirrored room.

Because the construction of *Infinity Mirror Room — Phalli's Field* was not completed until the day 'Floor Show' opened, a photograph of *My Flower Bed* was used on the publicity material, its vivid scarlet tones offering a perfect match for the red polka dots of the phallic field. For one photograph taken in her studio, Kusama wore a bright-red leotard and jacket that matched the vivid colour of *My Flower Bed* (fig.11). She curled up on the base of the 'plant', legs tucked underneath her body, eyes closed and one hand neatly folded underneath her head in a pantomime of sleep, calling to mind the psychotropic slumber of Dorothy in the film *The Wizard of Oz* (1939), as she slept in a field of red poppies, or perhaps even Francisco de Goya's famous etching and homage to artistic creativity *El sueño de la razón produce monstruos* (*The Sleep of Reason Brings Forth Monsters*, 1796—99; fig.23), in which the artist sleeps at his desk while the monsters of darkness and irrationality circle about him. In 1965 Kusama told an interviewer that she would 'curl up for the night in *My Flower Bed*', citing it as a source of comfort for the loneliness and anxiety she experienced after dark, but also referring to it as a threatening object, its flowers like those that 'trap insects in order to devour them'.[31] Such conceptual and formal ambiguity was at the heart of Kusama's practice, and found its fullest, all-encompassing expression in *Infinity Mirror Room — Phalli's Field*, a work in which reality and fantasy, comfort and discomfort, 'I' and 'other' become intimately entwined.

In her small photo-collage *Compulsion Furniture (Accumulation)* (c.1964; fig.14), Kusama pictured a similarly crammed and hectic environment to that offered by *Infinity Mirror Room — Phalli's Field*. The piece consists of a series of thickly layered, cut-out photographs of white *Accumulation* objects, glued together to produce an imaginary group shot of an impossibly crowded interior — a ghostly counterpart to the bright-red spotted interior of her mirrored environment. A casually dressed Kusama leans against the back of a chair, the sleeves of her oversized white shirt rolled up, her hair roughly clipped back: the hard-working artist pausing for a moment amidst a sea of her own creations. This image, pasted just off-centre, serves as a visual anchor to the otherwise seamless *mise en scène*. Briony Fer has suggested that, by including herself in the photo-collage, Kusama 'performs or stages herself as a subject'.[32] In this arrangement, space and scale are collapsed into one homogeneous surface, in which the forms press and crowd on each other with not a spare millimetre of ground visible beneath the phalanx of phallic forms. The crowded intensity of the scenario is emphasised to dramatic effect, for there is no way all these objects could occupy the same space, as presented in the collage. The question, perhaps, is precisely what kind of subject is here proposed, as Kusama's image appears to drift among the impossible sea of forms — both a part of the scenario and at the same time not quite fitting in.

Kusama 'maximises' the surface effect of her phallic-studded objects through the excessive colonisation of their surfaces and their subsequent redoubling.[33] A photograph taken in her studio around 1963 makes this point keenly. Kusama stands at the centre of her crowded loft, a macaroni-covered suitcase in each hand, as the drooping stem of *My Flower Bed* looms menacingly above her, the stuffed red fingers of the glove-leaves just stroking her shoulder and hair. At her feet is an amorphous mound of phallic bumps (at the bottom left corner of the image), while from the wall a series of reliefs protrudes, fat fingers that poke out and spread into the room. Only a small section of the floor is uncovered, and the photograph's close cropping communicates a claustrophobic and pressured environment. Objects and surfaces appear to blur with one another in the starkly lit scenario, as though each were part of the other: Kusama's dark outfit morphs with the background, and her patterned tights and the textured weft of her fur coat echo the web-like collage of circular stickers that is propped against a mounted wall relief at bottom right. Kusama poses here as the new arrival to a strange and unfamiliar world — the suitcases reminding us of her nomadic status as a newly arrived visitor to the US. She stands immersed in this crammed and chaotic environment that, while clearly of her own making, also reads as an allegory of her alien status in her newly adopted homeland.

Upon her arrival in New York City in 1958, one of the first things Kusama remembers doing was visiting the top of the Empire

State Building. Looking down on the city from this vantage point, Kusama claims this as the moment she decided she was going to become a famous artist.[34] Given that Kusama had only just moved to the United States from Japan a year earlier, could speak hardly any English and was armed only with a few words of advice from the painter Georgia O'Keefe, to whom Kusama had written some months previously to ask advice about how to make it as an artist in the US, her ambition appears in hindsight to have been astronomically high.[35] However, in a short period of time she was to exceed her own expectations. Within a few years she was garnering much attention in both the art press and popular media, with her environments and public happenings featuring naked, painted male and female performers. As she actively competed with Andy Warhol for media exposure, her headline-grabbing happenings ensured her the reputation she aggressively pursued.[36] It was, however, to be a short-lived career in the US, as her star (and health) quickly began to wane, and, in 1973, after a few years of itinerant living around Europe, Kusama returned to Japan, where she has lived since.[37]

After *Infinity Mirror Room — Phalli's Field* was installed, Kusama arranged for a series of photographs featuring her body nestled in the phallic field.[38] In one Kusama lies in the bed of squashy forms, arms outstretched, her slight frame sinking into the soft flooring (fig.1). Her head touches a mirrored wall on one side, while her legs stretch out toward the middle of the room, creating an uncanny mirrored double of her body that extends beyond the physical limits of the small room and all the way to 'infinity'. In another photograph from the same shoot, she stands in the red and white phallic field, arms folded behind her head, feet planted firmly on the soft floor, in a gesture that is part authoritative and part sexual (fig.2). In all the photographs Kusama wears the same bright-red leotard and leggings, a perfect match for the sea of red polka dots with which she appears to merge.

In another photograph taken inside her studio the year before *Infinity Mirror Room — Phalli's Field*, Kusama, wearing a black leotard and fishnet tights, clings to one of the floor panels, face pressed into the phallic field, her hands reaching forward to clasp the soft spotted cotton tuber as she glances coquettishly back at the camera. Kusama presents the object as both infant-like toy and abstract body part, playfully highlighting the conceptual and bodily slippages the forms suggest. In Mignon Nixon's words, Kusama here 'poses the phallus'.[39] Grasping the satisfyingly chubby protuberance as she looks straight out of the frame, Kusama demonstrates one way by which the 'phallus' can be mastered, and invites viewers to read her gesture as sexual. Once placed inside the mirrored room and laid flat on the floor, the panels of the 'phallic field' flooring are reduced to a supporting role against which Kusama takes centre stage — as does, by extension, the viewer, as participant.

In another photograph from 1965, taken by Eikoh Hosoe, Kusama sprawls across the floor of *Infinity Mirror Room — Phalli's Field* in a white leotard, legs bare and long hair tousled to frame her heavily made-up face (fig.4). In this image, Kusama emphasises the sexual nature of her presence among the 'groping protuberances'.[40] With her head tilted back, she looks up at the camera, her back arched and legs outstretched in a classic sex-kitten pose. She might be thought to parody the phallus (or to 'burlesque' it, as Nixon has noted); her knowing gesture allows her to assert control over the room's phallic visual regime.[41]

Infinity Mirror Room — Phalli's Field is not a work that fits easily into histories of the 1960s New York art world. It sits somewhat awkwardly between the Pop-like and the surreal, the minimal and the metaphorical, the figurative and the abstract, the psychotic and the erotic. *Infinity Mirror Room — Phalli's Field* is striking for the way in which it appears, on the one hand, like a somewhat hammy representation of what we might think the 1960s 'looked like', with its references to Pop art and psychedelia, and, on the other, for its absolute refusal to fit with the art scene of that period. Kusama both worked with and against the contemporary milieu, addressing in various ways the burgeoning Minimalist object, the explosion of Pop art across the US and Europe and the return to a form of post-War 'surrealism' that had been gaining visibility since the mid-1950s. Her work — even her large abstract canvases — were produced in direct conflict with modernist discourse that privileged the visual encounter over other kinds of engagement with art and its environment.

Alongside its psycologically charged aspects, Kusama's works offer other ways of thinking, experiencing and encountering not only the work of art, but also the world in which the object — and we as subjects — lives. It is my argument that within *Infinity Mirror Room — Phalli's Field* an idiosyncratic world is presented, which we are invited to imaginatively inhabit, albeit for a brief time. The psychological charge of Kusama's work may function to an extent as a kind of self-administered or reparative treatment for the artist, but reading it exclusively in those terms would miss the point. *Infinity Mirror Room — Phalli's Field* is not simply the articulation of one artist's 'interior' world, no more than it is merely a playful, kitsch funhouse. On the contrary, *Infinity Mirror Room — Phalli's Field* speaks to an engagement with the world at large, and the relations that occur within it.

It was not until the 1990s that curators and critics began to re-evaluate Kusama's contribution to the avant-garde scene of the 1960s. With the rise of interest in women artists whose work had been similarly sidelined, her activity as an artist and, latterly, author began to attract critical attention from art historians, critics and curators. They attended in particular to the gendered and psychoanalytically charged aspects of her practice, for, despite her vexed relationship with feminism, Kusama remains an artist whose work opens up questions of gender and sexuality in extraordinary ways.[42] I too want to attend to these aspects of Kusama's work, not in order to recuperate for her practice a feminism that was for the most part not there to begin with. Nor do I want to ignore the debilitating psychological conditions under which she has worked her whole life. Though these are important currents running through her practice, I do want to insist that these readings don't do full justice to *Infinity Mirror Room — Phalli's Field* as a theoretical and material object.[43] There are other interpretative frameworks through which I want to explore *Infinity Mirror Room — Phalli's Field*, for its critical power lies as much in the moments in which this work resists as in those in which it participates in the discourses of contemporary art.

Play and Performing the Self

Infinity Mirror Room — Phalli's Field, like much of Kusama's work from this time, was never sold. Instead, it was dismantled after the exhibition closed. The sections of polka-dotted flooring, which had already been used in a number of Kusama's photographs prior to the room's creation, were repurposed in her later happenings. Her first such public performance using the phallus-covered floor panels was the *14th Street Happening*, which took place in New York City in 1966, on the street outside her loft: Kusama climbed on and off the soft bed of polka dot forms, activating the sea of red and white by once again adding her body to its 'phallic field', as passers-by watched (fig.16). By placing the spotted flooring outside, on the sidewalk, rather than within the claustrophobic mirrored interior of *Infinity Mirror Room — Phalli's Field*, Kusama inserted her work into the everyday space of the city — or, to borrow an expression from the artist Allan Kaprow, she sought to 'blur' the boundaries between 'art' and 'life'. This 'blurring' was something Kaprow and artists such as Robert Rauschenberg had been striving to achieve since the mid-1950s.[44] Kaprow's group happenings and Rauschenberg's *Combines* — part-collage, part-junk assemblages — both drew on the motif of the 'everyday' in their three-dimensional expansion of the possibilities of painting. Kusama's happening similarly posed a disruption to the everyday activities of the street. Passers-by would find themselves arrested by the peculiar sight of a young woman alternately lying on the street and on the soft phallic bed of tubers. Photographs of the work show pedestrians keeping a wide berth as they observe Kusama's movements somewhat curiously (others it seems simply walked on by). After rearranging herself on the ground, Kusama would lie perfectly still as Hosoe captured her activities on film. In an inversion of how *Infinity Mirror Room — Phalli's Field* functions, Kusama placed the phallic field, her 'infinite wonderland' as she called it,[45] outside in the world. Instead of the red leotard Kusama wore for the photographs at Richard Castellane Gallery in 1965, for *14th Street Happening* Kusama lay prone and exposed on the ground, in a demure black dress with her hair in pig-tails.

Two years later, in August 1968, Kusama staged another outdoor happening in New York City's Central Park, which drew explicitly on Lewis Carroll's *Alice's Adventures in Wonderland* novel (1865). As part of her *Anatomic Explosion, a series of Happenings*, Kusama and a troupe of naked dancers climbed on top of the bronze *Alice in Wonderland* sculpture by José de Creeft that had been installed in the park in 1959 as a gift to the city's children, shortly after Kusama herself had arrived in Manhattan.[46] The happening, at which tea was served free of charge, was heavily orchestrated and publicised, with several bemused members of the press in attendance. The dancers, wearing nothing but masks of Richard Nixon, Fidel Castro,

Jackie Kennedy and a pig's head, danced and posed around the sculpture as Kusama painted their bodies with a series of multicoloured polka dots.[47] Despite its putatively political commentary (in which the contemporary political situation is likened to the absurd rules governing Alice's famous tea party), in the press release for *Alice in Wonderland Happening* Kusama explicitly linked the use of mirrors in her work with Alice's fictional adventures through the looking glass.[48] This took on a markedly psychedelic spin, with Kusama dubbing Alice the 'grandmother of the hippies' and herself a mix of the Mad Hatter and Alice.[49] In this happening Kusama presented herself as insider and outsider, passive observer and active participant, sane and insane — physical and psychological states around which she frequently organised her work.

One year after she first showed *Infinity Mirror Room — Phalli's Field*, Kusama produced a hexagonal-shaped room titled *Kusama's Peep Show — Endless Love*, in which the soft, spongy, spotted forms were substituted by hundreds of multicoloured spotlights, studded into the mirrored ceiling and walls and flashing at a furious speed. In this instance, viewers were not allowed to enter the room, but only to peer in through one of two letterbox-shaped peepholes placed directly opposite one another, so that they found themselves cast as voyeurs, trapped not only by the endless reflections but also by the gaze of another subject peering in (fig.18). Although Kusama later staged a group happening inside the room for the 1968 *Self-Obliteration* film, shot by Jud Yakult, the room is best known through carefully composed photographs featuring Kusama alone inside, clad in red and reclining on the floor, her brightly lit body split and refracted by the mirrored walls (fig.19). The aim of the room, it is clear, was to physically exclude visitors' bodies. What Kusama liked about this mirrored room in particular was the implicit tease of participation it offered, 'because it allows you to see things that you cannot touch'.[50] Kusama had first become interested in working with mirrors after a visit to the studio of Christian Megert in Switzerland in 1965. She saw his small, complex mirrored boxes and wall reliefs and, upon her return to New York, began work on *Infinity Mirror Room — Phalli's Field*. Megert's psychologically charged mirror pieces had been included in the large exhibition of artists from the Dutch Nul Group and the German Zero Group at the Stedelijk Museum in Amsterdam in 1965, in which Kusama also participated.[51]

Claire Bishop has related the use of mirrors by artists such as Kusama during the 1960s and 70s to French psychoanalyst Jacques Lacan's famous observation that 'the literal act of reflection is formative of the ego', published in his 1949 essay 'The Mirror Stage as Formative of the I Function as Revealed in Psychoanalytic Experience'.[52] For Lacan, the first glimpse of self that is reflected in the mirror offers the young infant a fantasy image of herself as a distinct, autonomous subject, despite the reality that she has at that moment only fragmentary self-knowledge, for she has command neither of her motor skills nor of language. It is a decisive moment in that process of becoming a subject, an 'I'. Lacan's citation of Caillois's account of 'legendary psychasthenia' and the 'derealising effect of an obsession with space' could serve well as a description of the similarly obsessive 'derealising effects' of Kusama's *Infinity Mirror Room — Phalli's Field* and *Kusama's Peep Show*.[53] The 'mirror stage', as Lacan dubbed it, 'is a drama whose internal thrust is precipitated from insufficiency to anticipation'.[54] It is precisely within that shift between the experience of a lack and a promise of 'self' — from partiality to plenitude — that I want to situate the encounter given occasion to by *Infinity Mirror Room — Phalli's Field*. For, while readings of Kusama's work have tended to divide sharply between those that emphasise 'oceanic bliss' and those that stress 'claustrophobic horror', it is in fact the push and pull between the two that *Infinity Mirror Room — Phalli's Field* most compellingly stages.[55]

Since the early 1960s, commentators have picked up on the psychologically inflected ways in which Kusama has described her work. By mid-decade, this angle dominated almost all critical readings, from the description of her 'phallus barnacled easy chair' as 'psychotic art' by one critic in 1964, to Kusama's own frequently cited accounts of her psychological illness, which fuelled myths of artistic 'madness'.[56] In recent years, readings of Kusama's work have reconsidered it as less the output of a mentally ill subject and instead in terms of her strategic production of a psychologically charged encounter that is no longer irreducibly linked to her own psychological state. Both Mignon Nixon and Briony Fer have discussed Kusama's use of reiteration and the phallic form through a psychoanalytic language of disavowal, splitting, repetition and the part-object. Far from offering a diagnostic account of Kusama's working practice, such an approach extends the implications of that psychoanalytic language beyond mere autobiographical narrative to address the wider cultural and psychological sphere in which both viewer and art object are situated.[57] Rather than revealing herself as immersed in a process of disintegration of the psyche, Kusama demonstrates — *performs* — the unravelling logic of that process.

Nixon has written that Kusama's phallic forms belong to a broader shift in art practice in the 1950s and 60s, to which a number of artists contributed, including Louise Bourgeois and Eva Hesse. Both artists worked with latex and plaster and other materials to produce abstract yet insistently bodily works, through which ran an anarchic, absurd sense of humour, as comically bulbous forms variously suggest inflated, truncated and multiplied body parts. In such work meaning remains

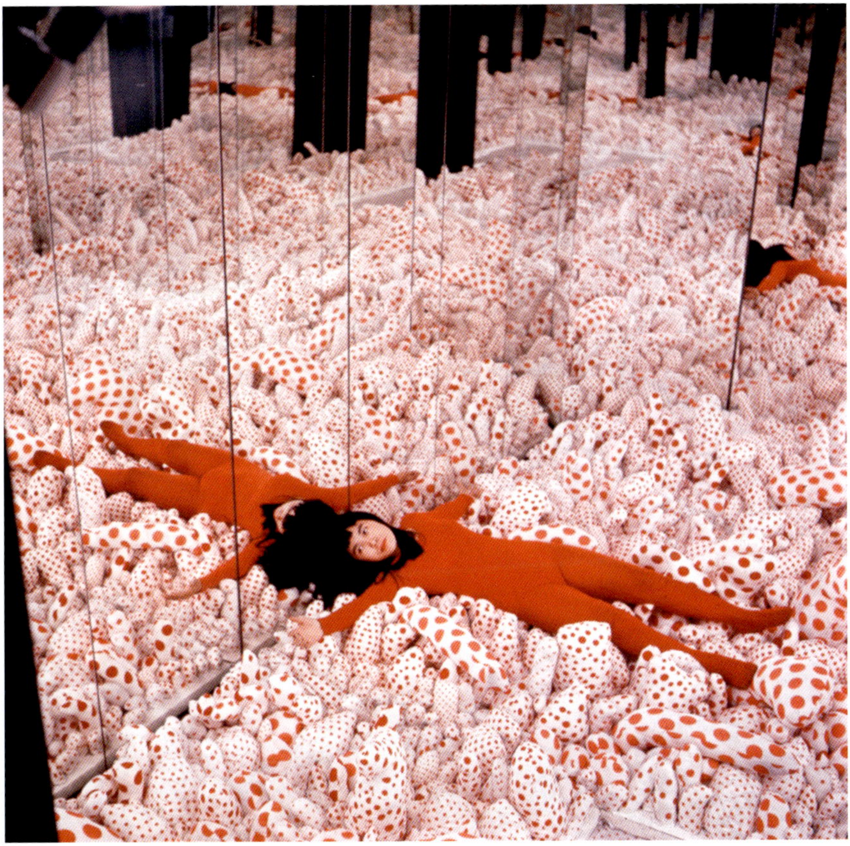

1. Yayoi Kusama,
Infinity Mirror Room — Phalli's Field, 1965,
sewn stuffed fabric, mirrors,
455 × 455 × 250cm,
installation view, Kusama lying on the floor, 'Floor Show', Richard Castellane Gallery, New York, 1965

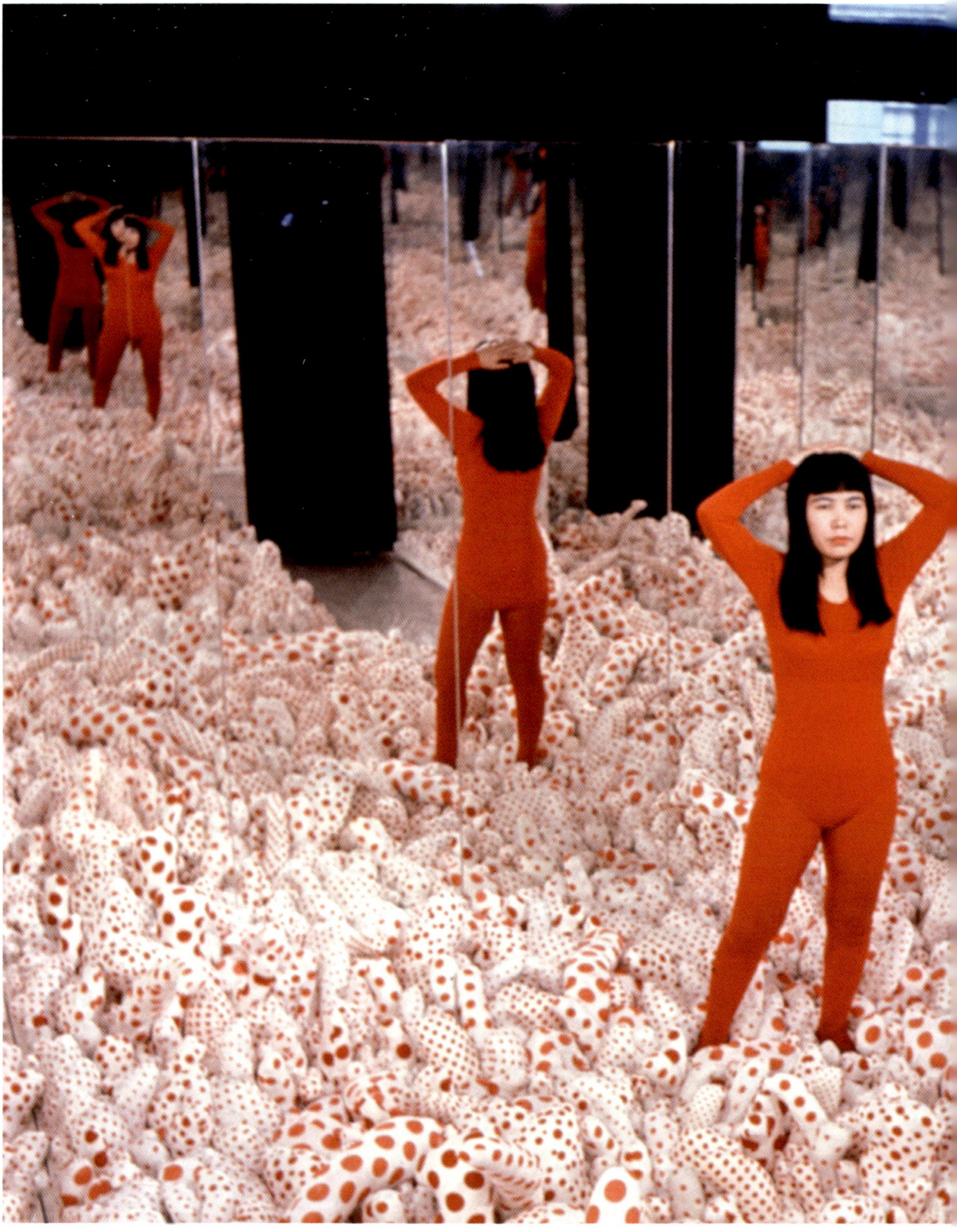

2. Yayoi Kusama standing inside
Infinity Mirror Room — Phalli's Field, 'Floor Show',
Richard Castellane Gallery, New York, 1965

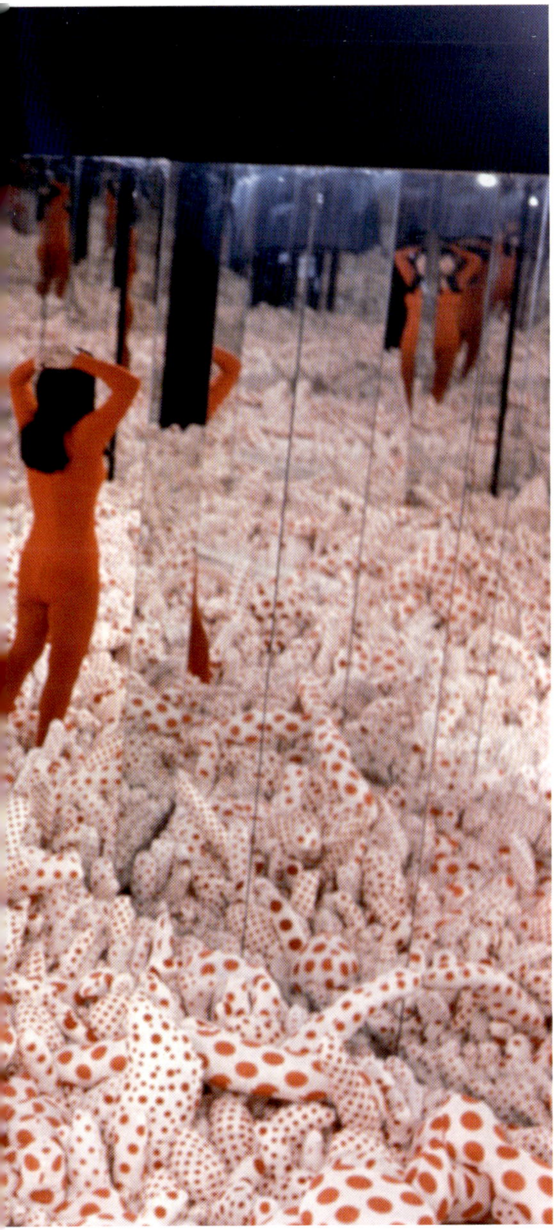

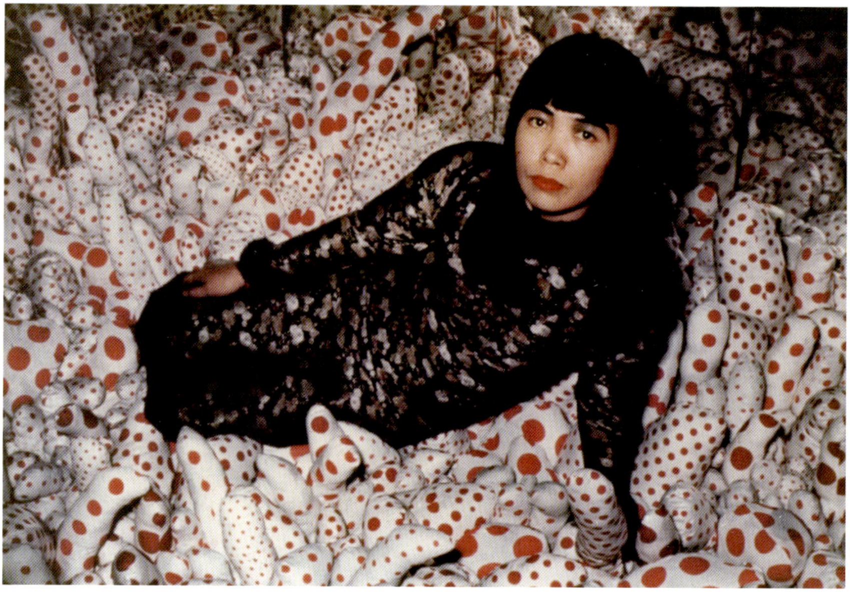

3. Yayoi Kusama lying on the floor of
Infinity Mirror Room — Phalli's Field,
'Floor Show', Richard Castellane Gallery,
New York, 1965

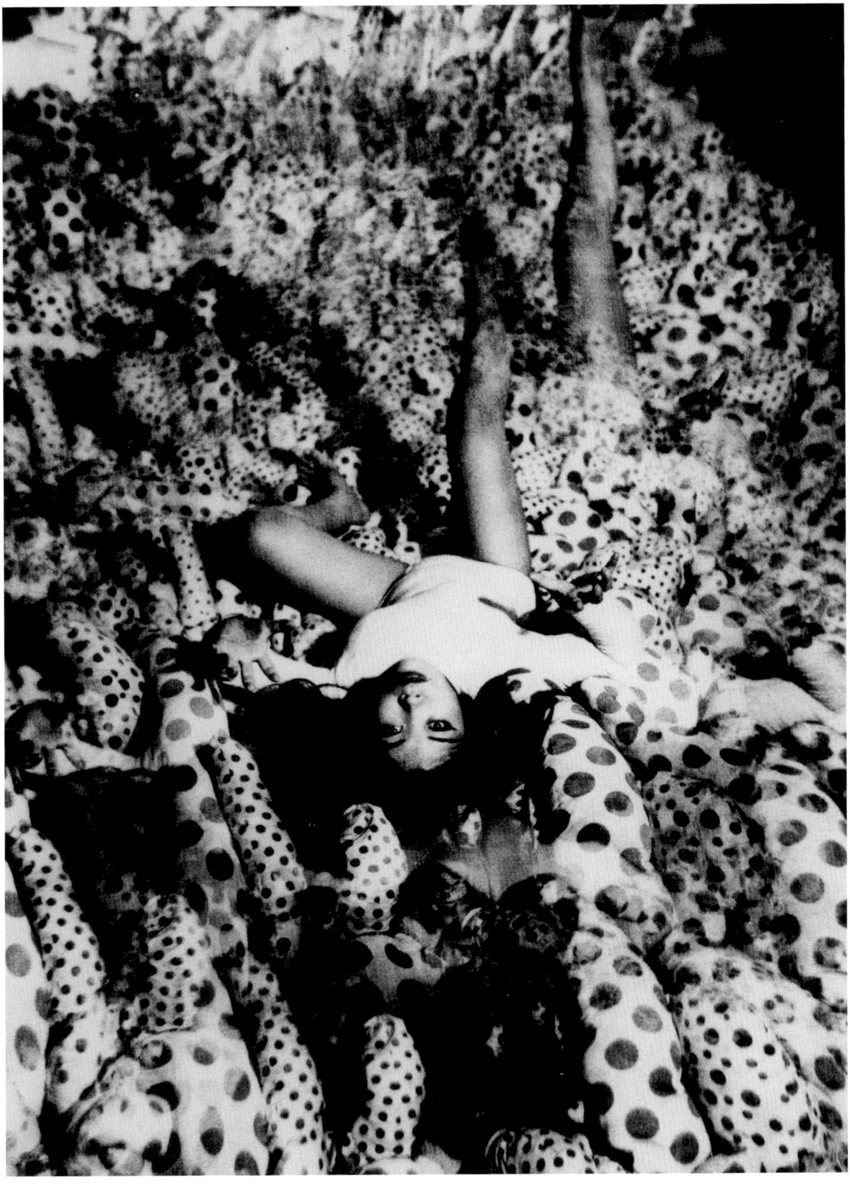

4. Yayoi Kusama lying on the floor of *Infinity Mirror Room — Phalli's Field*, 'Floor Show', Richard Castellane Gallery, New York, 1965
Photograph: Eikoh Hosoe

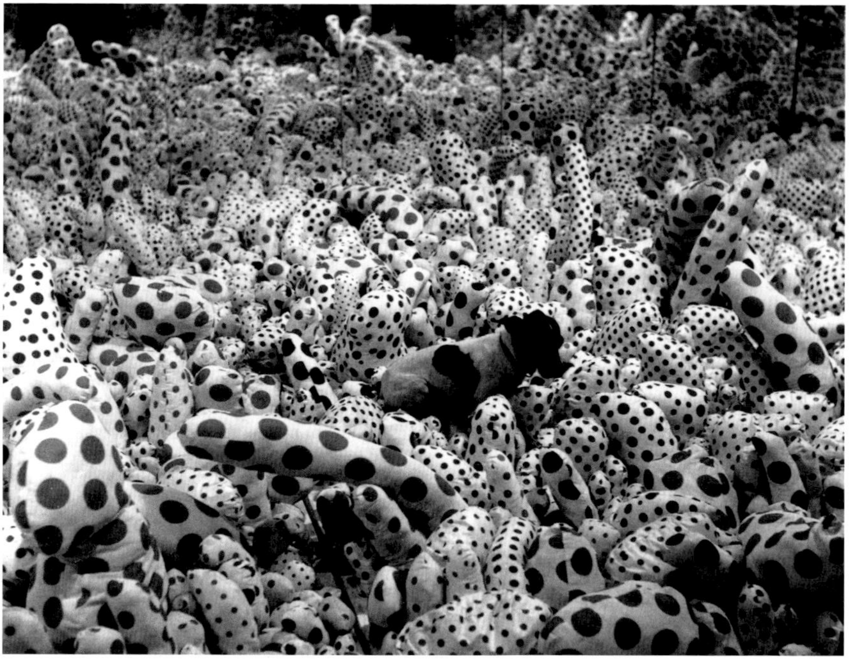

5. Spotted dog inside *Infinity Mirror Room — Phalli's Field*, 'Floor Show', Richard Castellane Gallery, New York, 1965

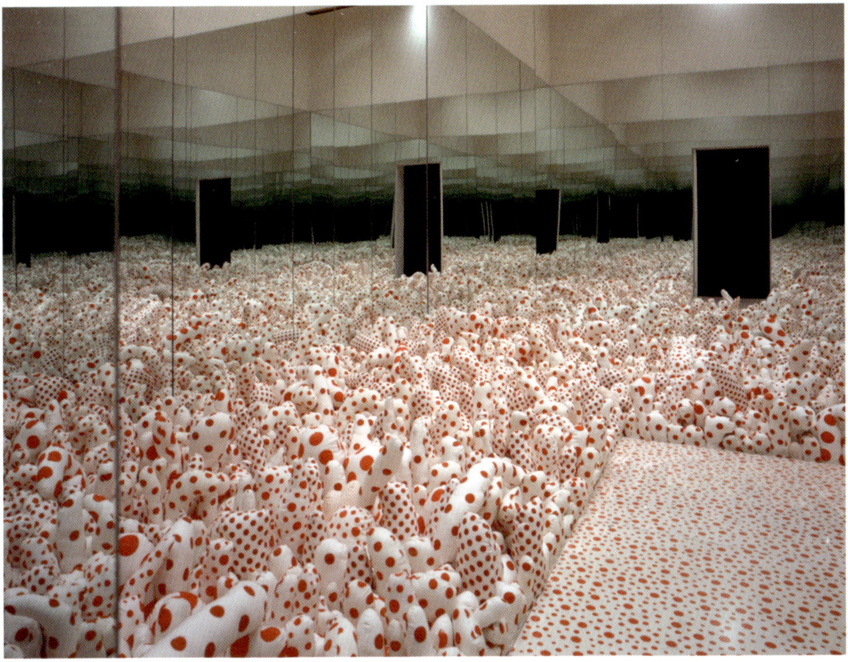

6. Yayoi Kusama,
Infinity Mirror Room — Phalli's Field,
reconstructed for 'Love Forever:
Yayoi Kusama 1958—1968',
Los Angeles County Museum of Art, 1998
Photograph: Norihiro Ueno

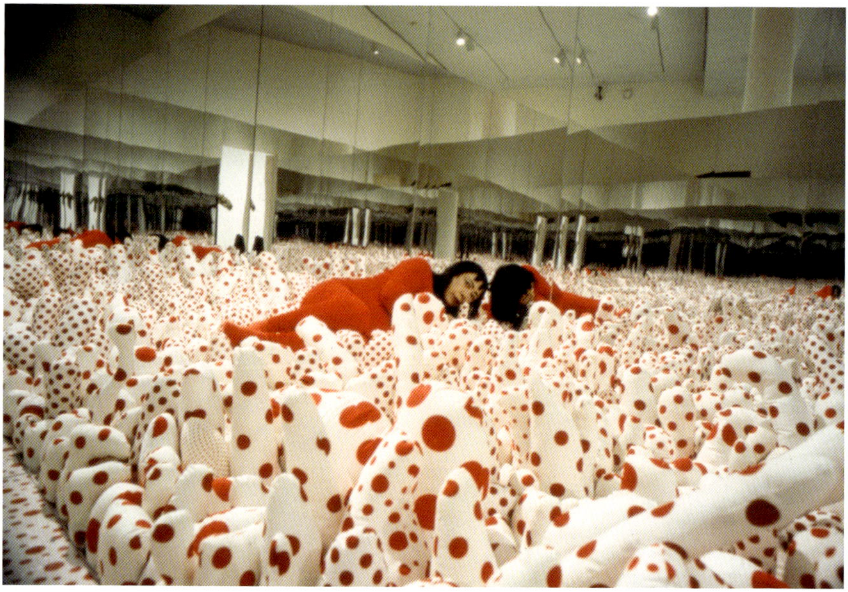

7. Yayoi Kusama lying on the floor of
Infinity Mirror Room — Phalli's Field,
'Love Forever: Yayoi Kusama 1958—1968',
Los Angeles County Museum of Art, 1998

mobile and the specific figuring of the 'body' is kept at arm's length. By employing processes of binding, wrapping and proliferation, both Bourgeois and Hesse, like Kusama with her stuffed tubers, enabled a mobility of form in which fantasies of the body — of the fantasised erotics of the body — are offered. Rather than understanding Kusama's 'phallic field' as a symptom of her anxieties about sex, as both critics and Kusama herself have presented it, her work might be viewed within the wider cultural and artistic milieu in which she was working, and with which her work was in dialogue at that time — from the Zero and Nul Groups in Europe that she showed with in the 1960s, to the work of her peers, including Hesse, and their renegotiation of the representation of the body. Kusama, Hesse and Bourgeois actively engaged with new ways of representing the body, of deflating the power of the phallic form through absurdist strategies of repetition and doubling — 'lost in its proliferation and dispersal' across the surface.[58] In so doing, they inject a subversive notion of play into the work that does not replace, but, on the contrary, underscores the polymorphously perverse aspect of her work — Freud's term for a mobile form of infantile sexuality in which erotic pleasure is taken from any part of the body.[59]

In his 1967 article 'Playing: A Theoretical Statement', D.W. Winnicott offered a reflection on his years of experience as an analyst working with young children.[60] For Winnicott, imaginative, creative play is essential to the young infant, who is unable to communicate with words. But play is for him also foundational to the psychological development of adult subjects. The 'potential space' in which play takes place is, Winnicott suggests, a cultural and psychological environment in which the young infant learns how to act and how to be in the world. The objects with which he or she plays in this space are dubbed 'transitional objects'; they can range from soft children's toys to comfort blankets. Playing with these objects the child learns how to mediate his or her relationship to the world. For Winnicott, it is the material world of things that is formative of the infant's sense of self, rather than his or her later entry into the symbolic realm of language, as Lacan maintained. He identified this 'potential space' as providing a safe environment in which the infant is able to loosen and play with the boundaries of self and other, to test what is real and what is fantasy, to learn how to negotiate and understand his or her position as subject. When Winnicott described play as 'a basic form of living', he offered, too, a productive model for thinking about how *Infinity Mirror Room — Phalli's Field* functions as a 'potential space' of creative play, providing all subjects — not just children — an arena in which to encounter the world and its objects, where the usual boundaries between what is real and what is not (those reflections, those repetitions) are momentarily relaxed in a freeing manner.[61]

From *Infinity Nets* to Minimalism

Kusama was already investigating psychological unease and the loosening of boundaries between, on the one hand, self and other and, on the other, subject and object in the *Infinity Net* paintings she began producing in 1958 (fig.8 and 9). In these she employed serial repetition and abstraction to articulate a fracture of the psyche and sense of endlessness. These paintings were also her first serious foray into experimenting with the spatial parameters of the room and with techniques for expanding and contracting that space in order to generate a mobile and disorienting environment. The surfaces of the *Infinity Net* paintings comprise hundreds of thick, stubby interlocking licks of paint that conjoin into a continuous lateral spread. The 'net' is set afloat above a painted ground that variously contrasts with or almost matches the colour of the floating web. In her first *Infinity Net* paintings, Kusama overlaid two barely contrasting shades of cream and white. Colour quickly crept in, as she began to produce slightly smaller *Infinity Net* paintings featuring green, red and yellow polka dots or 'nets' over backgrounds of black, white or gold. In other versions of the paintings (which she returned to in the 1990s and continues to produce today), the endless loops are substituted for hundreds of acid-bright acrylic fields of bubbles, polka dots or nets that stand out starkly as a series of punctuating marks or 'holes'. To make her *Infinity Nets* Kusama invested a huge amount of physical labour, crouching over canvases, oftentimes large, for hours on end, obsessively applying globby curls of creamy oil paint to the surface. The gauzy shimmer effect that the paintings produce from a distance comes undone on closer inspection, as the streaks and clots of paint are strikingly material and viscous — like the 'waddling fungal growths' that protruded fantastically from the yellow wallpaper in Gilman's story.

By allowing the painted nets to spread out, like veils, right up to the edge of their stretched, unframed canvases, the *Infinity Nets* suggest continuity beyond the physical limits of the support. Standing in front of the early paintings (the longest of which measures 10 metres; fig.9) is a dizzying experience, whether one looks up close at the individual brush marks or views them from afar, as the individually rendered marks merge into one continuous or 'infinite' field of barely-differentiated colour, texture and tone.[62] Kusama's net paintings attracted critical attention straight away, with reviewers picking up on their originality, recognising the new and complicated relationship the *Infinity Nets* established with both the avant-gardist strategy of the monochrome and the gestural style of the Abstract Expressionists. Descriptions ranged from highlighting the obsessive, neurotic and vertiginous aspect of the works, to underlining them as austere and materialist objects (as Donald Judd did).[63] Like the mirrored reflections of the phallic tubers and visitors' bodies inside *Infinity Mirror Room — Phalli's Field*, the *Infinity Nets* refuse to cohere or let up in their relentless insistence on a kind of endlessness that is at once exhilarating in its promise and confusing in its implications — where does the work, and the 'I' standing in its midst, begin or end, start or finish?

After Kusama's first show of the *Infinity Nets* at the Brata Gallery in New York in 1958, they were included in a number of international exhibitions, including Udo Kultermann's 'Monochrome Malerei' ('Monochrome Painting'), held at the Städtisches Museum in Leverkusen in 1960. This exhibition, which introduced the *Infinity Nets* to Europe, showed them alongside works by Lucio Fontana, Yves Klein, Heinz Mack, Piero Manzoni, Otto Piene, Günther Uecker and Robert Ryman. Uecker's pin-studded monochrome 'paintings' from the 1960s were dizzying in their appeal both visually and tactilely (as both inviting and dangerous three-dimensional objects), while Piene worked with light and movement to disrupt the kind of viewing encounter that a wall-mounted work typically offers. The Nouveau Réaliste artists in the exhibition worked less with the pristine items displayed in Pop art from the US than the detritus of a consumer society, piled, stacked or crammed together into dirty assemblages. Niki de Saint Phalle, among them, would shoot a rifle at white monochrome paintings, the surfaces of which hid containers filled with brightly coloured paint that would burst through the white surface, rupturing it with thick slicks of pigment. But while her *Tir*, or 'shooting paintings', appeared to reject outright the legacy of earlier abstract painters, for Kusama there remained something worth mining in that tradition — albeit via a language of ambiguity, obsession and serial repetition.[64]

So Kusama's painting practice fits fairly comfortably within a European tradition of abstraction. (Certainly her hyperbolic pronouncements sit well alongside the utopian claims of an earlier generation of abstract painters such as Kazimir Malevich and Aleksandr Rodchenko, albeit to very different ends.) But it was through her move into three dimensions that she established a formal visual language that was entirely her own. Despite the idiosyncrasies of the environments Kusama produced, inflected as they are with an air of psychological tension, they also set out to frame a kind of social process by bringing people together inside enclosures (sharing something with the environmental work of the Constructivists). In reviewing her *Infinity Net* paintings in 1959, Judd described them in relational terms, claiming that the formal relationships were not autonomous and self-contained across the surface of her 'complex and simple' paintings.[65] On the contrary, Judd saw Kusama's works as affecting not only the viewer's field of vision, but also the entire physical environment in which they and their viewers were situated. Kusama herself considered the paintings important precursors to her move into 'soft sculpture' in 1962:

> *The nets I was painting had continued to proliferate until they had spread beyond the canvas to cover the tables, the floor, the chairs and the walls. The result of the unlimited development of this obsessional art was that I was able to shed my painter's skin and metamorphose into an environmental sculptor.*[66]

As if to emphasise this point, in 1961 she posed for a photograph standing in front of one of her net paintings, a carefully composed shot in which the canvas is abruptly truncated at both ends (fig.9). The cropped photograph gives the impression that the painted surface expands and spreads indefinitely. In fact, in 1964 she described her *Infinity Net* paintings as 'without composition — without beginning, end or centre'.[67]

For Judd, Kusama's *Infinity Net* paintings resembled not an iridescent web but rather 'a vigorously carved grill', or, in a description that comes closer to accounting for the thick licks of white interlocking loops, a sheet of 'massive, solid lace'.[68] Judd's interpretation of Kusama's paintings did not dwell on their status as dizzying and psychologically affective, but rather approached them as physical and material objects. While Kusama's early work, with its use of brightly coloured materials and engagement with everyday objects, belonged perhaps most straightforwardly to Pop and assemblage art, by the early years of the 1960s the emerging Minimalist object was on her radar, alongside the new forms of monochrome painting and object-making such as Piero Manzoni's *Achromes* (various canvases impregnated with gesso or kaolin and white reliefs made of polystyrene balls, fake fur, white painted dinner rolls, produced from 1959 to 1963) and Yves Klein's slick, rounded and wall-mounted monochrome panels painted in brilliant blue paint (a colour dubbed by the artist 'International Klein Blue', and first produced in 1955). Manzoni and Klein considered their 'monochromes' as much objects as paintings, as much ideas as things, and Kusama's *Infinity Nets* could also lay claim to this status. Her paintings, like Manzoni's and Klein's art, were a self-consciously fashioned response to contemporary abstract painting as much as they were outward articulations of her internal psychology — despite Kusama's claims to the contrary.

To many critics, Kusama's work appeared to offer an eccentrically absurd response to the Minimalists' repetitive forms and the stacking and ordering of identical units of everyday materials in their three-dimensional work. In place of Judd's aluminium, plywood and concrete, Kusama used fabric and foodstuffs. Even when employing the visual language of the monochrome and serial repetition, the multiples Kusama made were anthropomorphic, erotic and surreal. A key instance of Kusama's

'Minimalist' language was an environment she installed at the Gertrude Stein Gallery in 1963, titled *Aggregation: One Thousand Boats Show*, an early engagement with the Minimalist visual language that had recently emerged in the New York art world. Within the show, a large, white-painted rowboat (which Judd had helped Kusama carry back to her studio) was displayed in a room, with its walls and those of the adjacent corridor papered with 999 black-and-white photographic reproductions of the same boat. The repetition of this most ordinary object built up to a climax in which the actual 'thing' finally appeared at the end of the corridor, where the boat and oars were completely covered with white stitched fabric protuberances, forecasting the red spotted forms that would proliferate across the floor two years later in *Infinity Mirror Room — Phalli's Field*. The environment was presented less as an entire room than as a tableau organised from a frontal point of view — to be seen head-on.[69] The emphasis on the single object, even if repeated over and over, was close to the discrete, crammed *Accumulation* furniture and other items Kusama had spent the previous year producing, and did not yet fully aim at creating an all-encompassing installation, as *Infinity Mirror Room — Phalli's Field* would later do.

Kusama staged a series of photographic shoots inside *Aggregation: One Thousand Boats Show*, in which she posed naked, standing between the wall and boat, cranking up the psychosexual intensity of the room by accentuating the bodily implications of the 'phallic contour' of the boat and oars (fig.13).[70] Her monochrome spareness offered a playful and bodily rendering of form that was a far cry from the industrial materials and rigid geometric structures that Minimalist artists brought into the gallery space. In 1967 Michael Fried published his damning critique of Minimalism in a special issue of *Artforum* dedicated to contemporary sculpture, in which he attacked it for what he identified as 'theatricality'.[71] By this Fried meant the extent to which the Minimalist object could only be experienced in time — the time it takes to navigate its physical occupation of space, which he compared to how we navigate any object in a room (a table, a chair, other bodies...). For him, such an ordinary, everyday encounter with an object was the opposite of the aesthetic encounter artworks should offer (he was thinking of recent abstract paintings by Jules Olitski, or earlier by Jackson Pollock). Literally manoeuvring one's way around a series of grey-painted plywood polyhedra did not come anywhere near fulfilling his desire for a contemplative mode of engagement ('we are all literalists most or all of our lives', he complained, expecting art to offer us a fundamentally different kind of experience).[72] In contrast, the writing of Minimalist artists and critics, including Judd and Robert Morris (who was responsible for seven grey plywood polyhedra, installed in December 1964 at the Green Gallery),[73] heralded the everydayness of the Minimalist object — its obdurate resistance to the 'aesthetic' of high modernist criticism — as precisely the point. In his 1966 essay 'Notes on Sculpture Part Two', Morris had argued that what made Minimalism so distinctive was precisely the involvement of spectators within the environment in which the objects were situated. While in the following passage Morris describes the Minimalist object, his account holds true also for the kinds of affective engagement offered by *Aggregation: One Thousand Boats Show* and *Infinity Mirror Room — Phalli's Field*, which anticipated his claims for the Minimalist object:

> *The better new work takes relationships out of the work and makes them a function of space, light and the viewer's field of vision. The object is but one of the terms in the newer aesthetic. It is in some way more reflexive because one's awareness of oneself existing in the same space as the work is stronger than in previous work, with its many internal*

relationships. One is more aware than before that he himself is establishing relationships as he apprehends the object from various positions and under varying conditions of light and spatial context [...] *For it is the viewer who changes the shape constantly by his change in position relative to the work.*[74]

When Kusama posed with her monochrome boat, against the 'spatial context' of the photographic reproductions of that same boat papering the surrounding walls, she too made clear the extent to which the 'reflexive' aspect of her work, in which 'one's awareness of oneself existing in the same space as the work', was essential. By choosing to ratchet up the intensity of the relationship between subject and object as equally erotic, Kusama openly embraced the surreal, anthropomorphic and temporal aspects of *Aggregation: One Thousand Boats Show*, in which the spectacular effects of the environment and its tableau format placed the spectator at its centre. Of course it was precisely for such a theatrical framing of the artwork that Fried later attacked the Minimalist object. In embracing the theatrical as well as the Minimal in her room environments, Kusama signalled her burgeoning interests in performative and time-based art, which would, over the next few years, see her concerns diverge sharply from those of her Minimalist peers.

Domesticity and the Body

As well as engaging in an elliptical relationship with Minimalism, Kusama was aware of how her work might be understood in terms of gender, an aspect she explored via her staged presence in the environment of her phallic forms. With these photographs, she offered a sly riposte to the machismo of the contemporary art scene. This is not to say that she offered a 'feminine' alternative, but that she demonstrated the absurdity of attaching any kind of 'gendered' interpretation to abstract forms, highlighting their fundamentally slippery and polyvalent nature. Kusama was not alone in this critical reappraisal of abstraction, and, by the early 1970s, a number of women artists were explicitly engaging with these themes from a defiantly feminist perspective. Domesticity had, since the early 1960s, been a key theme of Kusama's work, as it placed pressure on the private sphere of 'women's work' to reveal it as a site of erotic drives, power and play. These themes returned with a heightened political edge in the 1970s, with a generation of artists for whom an ambivalent relationship to questions of gender would no longer suffice. For their vivid, vocal and highly politicised feminist agenda, the site of the domestic was a key battleground.

In 1971, 'Womanhouse',[75] the collaborative community project created by professors and students from the newly formed Feminist Art Program at the California Institute of the Arts (CalArts), transformed an old Hollywood mansion by converting each room into distinct art installations by individuals or groups of artists. Produced under the guidance of Miriam Shapiro and Judy Chicago, the rooms inside 'Womanhouse' included Chicago's now infamous *Menstruation Bathroom* (1972), a white space in which the only flash of colour was provided by the 'bloodied' sanitary towels that overflowed from the wastebasket, and Faith Wilding's *Crocheted Environment (Womb Room)* (1972), in which Wilding hung an enormous, creamy-white crocheted web from the ceiling and walls, as if a materialisation of Kusama's *Infinity Net* paintings. (But whereas Wilding sought to invoke a womb-like environment, Kusama sought to produce the opposite effect — she has frequently invoked her earliest traumas as stemming from a childhood spent under the exacting and cold upbringing of her mother in an environment that was far from nurturing and maternal.)[76] *Nurturant Kitchen* (1972) was the name of an installation by Robin Weltsch, which included Susan Frazier's *Aprons in Kitchen* (1972) and Vicki

Hodgetts's *Eggs to Breasts* (1972; fig.28). This imagery arose from a series of consciousness-raising meetings that took place in the kitchen space, during which the participants recalled painful incidences involving their mothers, the kitchen and food. But the playful and erotic undertones of the room, the humour lacing its construction, recall, too, the phallic protuberances of *Infinity Mirror Room — Phalli's Field*, as well as the polka dot saturation of Kusama's surfaces.

More recently, artists including Mona Hatoum and Rachel Whiteread have similarly investigated domesticity as a site of the psychological, the erotic and the deathly. Whiteread's play with the formal language of Minimalism has resulted in plaster and resin casts of the spaces between and around familiar domestic items, such as chairs and tables, rendered abstract in their serial, monochrome repetition. Hatoum's *Home* (1999) represents, like Kusama's '*Driving Image* Show', a domestic tableau of kitchen utensils laid out in a mock kitchen environment, on a long table (fig.29).[77] The household items (colander, pasta maker, light bulb, whisk) are connected by snaking tendrils of live electric cable, light bulbs fade up and down, and the sound of the rise and fall of electrical current is amplified, crackling and buzzing in a menacing way — the scenario is barricaded behind a fence of stretched wires, suggesting the domestic interior is a caged and dangerous space.

When Kusama's series of '*Driving Image* Show' exhibitions opened in the US, Italy and Germany from 1964 to 1966, they were installed to resemble similarly disrupted, chaotic and highly charged domestic interiors.[78] Although slightly different in each incarnation, the installations included a range of her recent furniture and other domestic items painted in vividly hued polka dots or colonised by clusters of fabric phalli, to function as a showcase of her work to date. The two rooms comprising the New York City installation were crammed full, resulting in an overwhelming, overstuffed, immersive environment. The first room contained a chaotic mix of dried macaroni-covered shop mannequins and a dresser, placed on a carpet of loosely strewn macaroni that cracked and crunched when stepped on. For the opening of the exhibition Kusama arranged for two 'macaroni-coated dogs' to be set loose, their 'frantic barking' startling viewers as the dogs began to 'dash around frantically, barking and weaving between the legs of high-heeled women who shrieked as they trod the macaroni floor'.[79] Part of the interior was turned into a kitchen and another into a dressing room. A female shop mannequin-cum-hostess, covered in macaroni, was placed in the centre of the multicoloured, riotous, polka dot-painted environment.

The room was intended to give 'concrete shape' to Kusama's ideas of obliteration, which 'emerged from the image of a tablecloth engulfing a telephone'.[80] The polka dot pattern of the tablecloth 'spilled over onto the telephone, climbed the door in the background and continued to proliferate, adhering to the walls and ceiling. The floor was wall-to-wall macaroni.'[81] For the installation at the Galerie M.E. Thelen in Essen (fig.20), a loud Beatles soundtrack filled the room, as though a radio were playing somewhere in the 'home' and adding an insistently contemporary air to the cacophony.[82] If feminism was a long way from Kusama's agenda in 1964, her violent attack on the standardised norms of the domestic interior was a powerful marker of resistance nonetheless: by inviting chaos and breakage, cacophony and confusion, Kusama's environmental installations did much to dismantle accepted codes of behaviour and notions of privacy and interiority. The traditional realm of the female subject was turned inside out, as private became public, order disorder and the usual way of going about things was turned dramatically on its head.

Eva Hesse and Claes Oldenburg similarly employed strategies of subversion in their soft sculptural objects — objects that suggest a notion of play (the 'transitional object', Winnicott noted, often takes the form of a 'soft toy').[83] While Kusama's work clearly involves her own personal experience, it also spoke directly to the emerging formal and conceptual concerns of Hesse and Oldenburg, as well as Lucas Samaras, Jackie Winsor and Louise Bourgeois. When, in the mid-1960s, Lucy Lippard dubbed the work of these and others as 'abstract-erotic', she grouped their work alongside Kusama's own witty play between soft and hard, animate and inanimate.[84] Hesse's collection of shiny black sausage forms in *Several* (1965), or the equally phallic appearance of *Ingeminate* (1965), with its cord-wrapped black allantoid volumes conjoined by a length of surgical rubber hose, offer the absurd suggestion of part-objects recast as playthings shot through with sexual language. Like Kusama's proliferation of phallic forms, the long thin forms of *Several* allude to and at the same time spiral away from the 'phallus' as single entity, to present instead a fantasy of the part-object as a series of playful substitutes.[85] In one memorable photograph, Hesse stands holding the two squat tubers of *Ingeminate*, grinning at the gesture in which the single phallic form is doubled into a pair of curiously humorous objects (fig.26). The conflation of Hesse's body with her work, like Kusama's *blurring* of herself with her work, suggests an empathetic response in which the work somehow 'mirrors' or mimics a particular model of 'self'. As Amelia Jones has noted, one of the most basic conundrums posed by Kusama's work is 'am I an object? Am I a subject?'[86] Clearly there is a psychological as well as erotic economy at work in her art, as questions of subjectivity and agency are foregrounded to unexpected ends. Both Kusama and Hesse place pressure on familiar habits of viewing and thinking about the body.

Hesse's play with repetition was shared by Oldenburg's soft renderings of everyday domestic and food items, which were often oversized and redoubled, such as his vinyl *Four Dormeyer Blenders* (1967), complete with drooping soft whisks, and his burlap and plaster *Two Cheeseburgers, with Everything* (1962). For Bourgeois, latex rather than fabric provided the material means to convey a sense of bodily softness, disintegration and collapse with her sculptural work of the 1960s. In *Le Regard* (*The Gaze*, 1966; fig.27), her confusion and intermingling of body parts — perhaps genitals, gaping mouths or staring eyes — insists, like Kusama's phallic-field of white protuberances, on the changeable and precarious status of objects that register on the one hand as sexually charged and on the other as infantile and funny. There is, however, an innocence, or perhaps naivety, to Kusama's joyous field of squashy protuberances, to which Bourgeois's and Hesse's works never quite yield. Like Kusama, both artists were photographed variously holding, supporting or enveloped in the materials of their work. In one witty and knowing photograph taken by Hermann Landshoff, Hesse lies on a low sofa with a tangle of ropes over her body, as though she were tied and bound to the analyst's couch.[87] In the photographs of these artists with their work, they frequently appear grinning broadly, slyly and, above all, knowingly, as they perform for the camera the subversive logic of their work, drawing attention to the bodily and libidinal charge of their abstract objects.

Lee Lozano's series of drawings from around 1963 and 1964 similarly revelled in self-consciously conjoining body parts, from penises and vaginas to breasts and mouths, in absurd formations underlined by savage humour. In Lozano's untitled drawings box-like containers hold an array of mismatched limbs and genitals, presenting an erotically charged assault on how we think of the body as an assemblage of desiring, devouring part-objects that offers no possibility of safe respite. In one drawing, a squat penis bursts from the palm of an outstretched hand, while in another breasts, penises and vaginas are snugly compartmentalised in a shoebox. In *No Title* (1964; fig.25), the phallic form takes on the Minimalist, yet abstract-erotic appearance of a workshop tool, caught somewhere between erect phallus and drill bit.[88]

In 1966 Lucy Lippard labelled the new tendency toward working with abstract-erotic forms and materials 'eccentric abstraction', on the occasion of an exhibition of the same name that she organised at the Fischbach Gallery in New York.[89] The exhibition included work by Bourgeois, Hesse, Alice Adams, Gary Kuehn, Bruce Nauman, Don Potts, Keith Sonnier and Frank Lincoln Viner. While Lippard considered Kusama an important 'abstract-erotic' artist, due to her combination of the surreal and the Minimal, Kusama and by extension artists such as Lozano were excluded from the exhibition on the grounds that for all their 'eccentricity' they remained committed to figuration. What Kusama did provide, according to Lippard, was a groundbreaking use of materials that heralded a new formal and material vocabulary for abstract artists, including soft, squashy, ephemeral and skin-like objects, contrasting with the monumental and unyielding media employed by Minimalist artists.
In fact, Lippard explicitly declared the works in her show not in opposition to but in critical dialogue with Minimalism.
For, as Lippard and others have noted, the shiny reflective sheen of Judd's plexiglas cubic structures and Morris's *Mirror Cubes* (1965) can just as readily be described in terms of the processes of psychological splitting and narcissistic desire they engender (for example, the endless reflections caused between Morris's four mirrored cubes) and the tactile nature of their surfaces.[90]
Among Lippard's selection of works that appeared to subvert the logic of Minimalism was Kuehn's *Melt Piece* (1966), a white, rectangular fibreglass sculpture that appears to 'melt' at the

edges, pooling into a puddle of hardened fibreglass on the floor in an amusingly literal undoing of Minimalism's geometric rigour. This and the other works registered as open instead of complete; they seemed in part constituted by the encounter with the viewer — an empathetic, erotic encounter that was the obverse of the 'literalist' mode of encounter that Michael Fried critiqued the Minimalists for maintaining.

'Become one with your environment'

In 1967, the 'abstract-erotic' phallic carpet of *Infinity Mirror Room — Phalli's Field* was redeployed to provide the backdrop for the series of what Kusama called her 'naked body painting happenings', in which she painted nude men and women with polka dots as they cavorted in front of a film camera under her direction. In 1968 the room's cushioned floor panels were again repurposed, this time as wall panels before which naked performers participated in Kusama's *Homosexual Happening* (fig.21). By introducing naked bodies into the room, Kusama was able to playfully literalise the abstract spotted 'phallic field'. With this and other happenings, such as *Grand Orgy to Awaken the Dead at the MoMA — Featuring Their Usual Display of Nudes* (1969), which took place in the New York museum's sculpture garden, or *Naked Protest at Wall Street, New York* (1968), in which four naked participants danced to the sound of bongo drums while Kusama sprayed them with polka dots (the police quickly closed the event down), she revelled in the chaotic arrangement of nudes, clustering them together into groups as they 'performed' for the ever-present camera. Kusama privileged group participation in these events, parsed through a language of freedom, open expression and sexual liberation.

The Wall Street protest, in particular, offered her starkest political statement, with the accompanying press release denouncing the stock market as 'capitalist bullshit'. As well

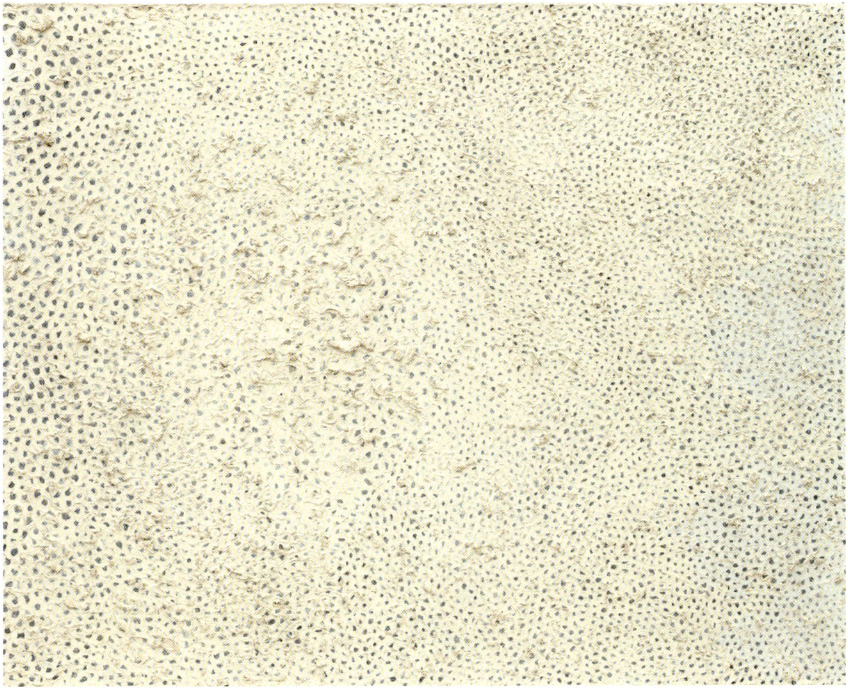

8. Yayoi Kusama,
No. F, 1959,
oil on canvas,
105.4 × 132.1cm
digital image © 2012 The Museum of Modern
Art, New York/Scala, Florence

9. Yayoi Kusama with a 10-metre *Infinity Net* painting, Stephen Radich Gallery, New York, 1961

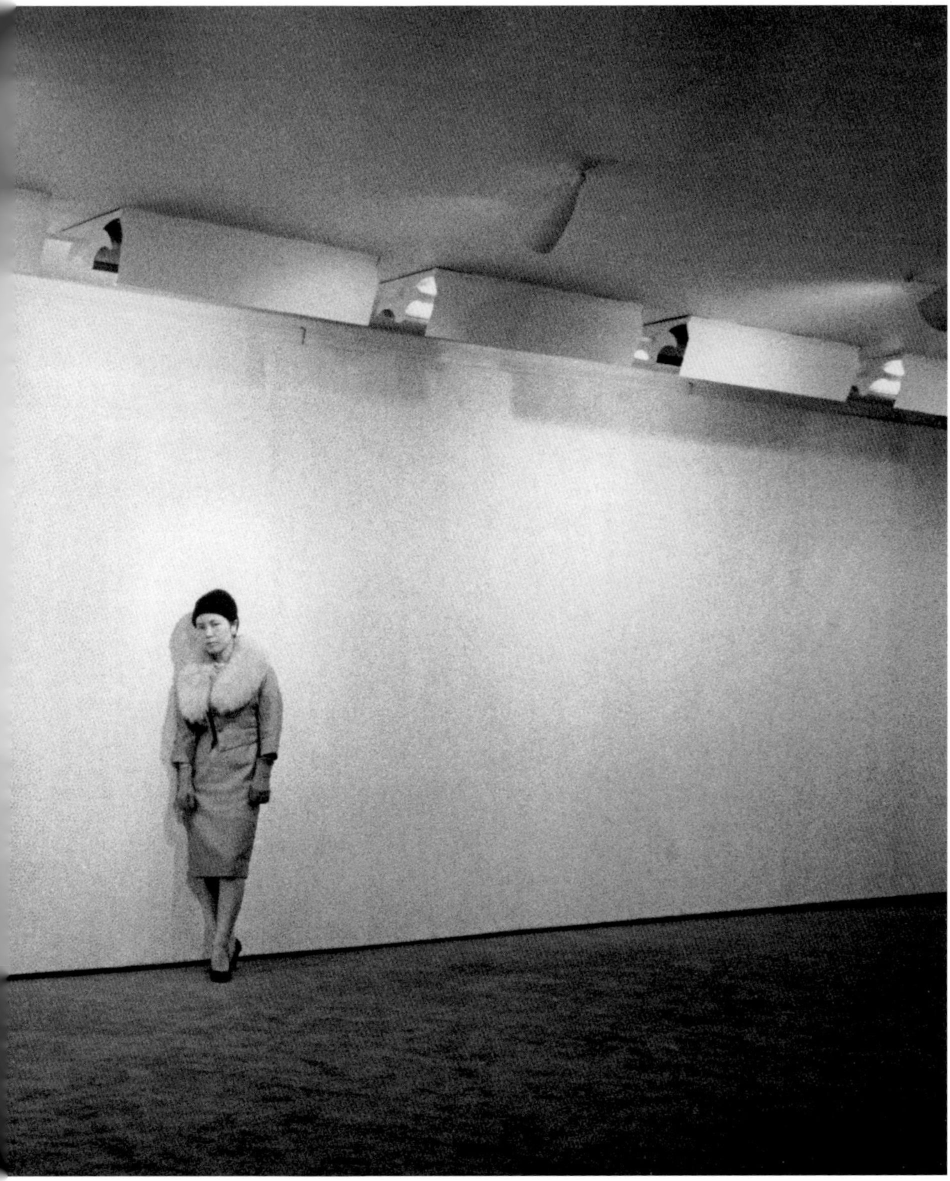

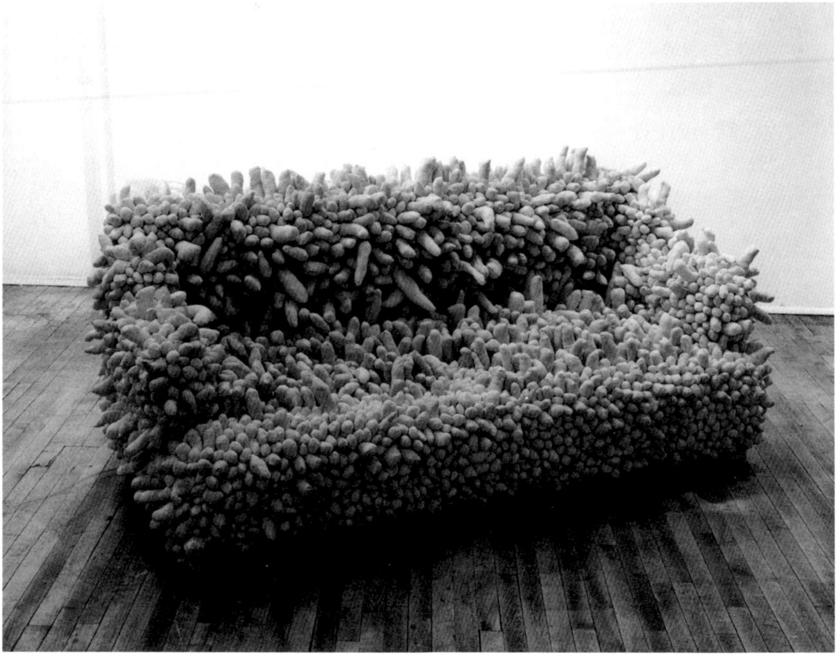

10. Yayoi Kusama,
Accumulation 2, 1962,
sofa frame, stuffed fabric, plaster and paint,
89 × 223.5 × 102.3cm

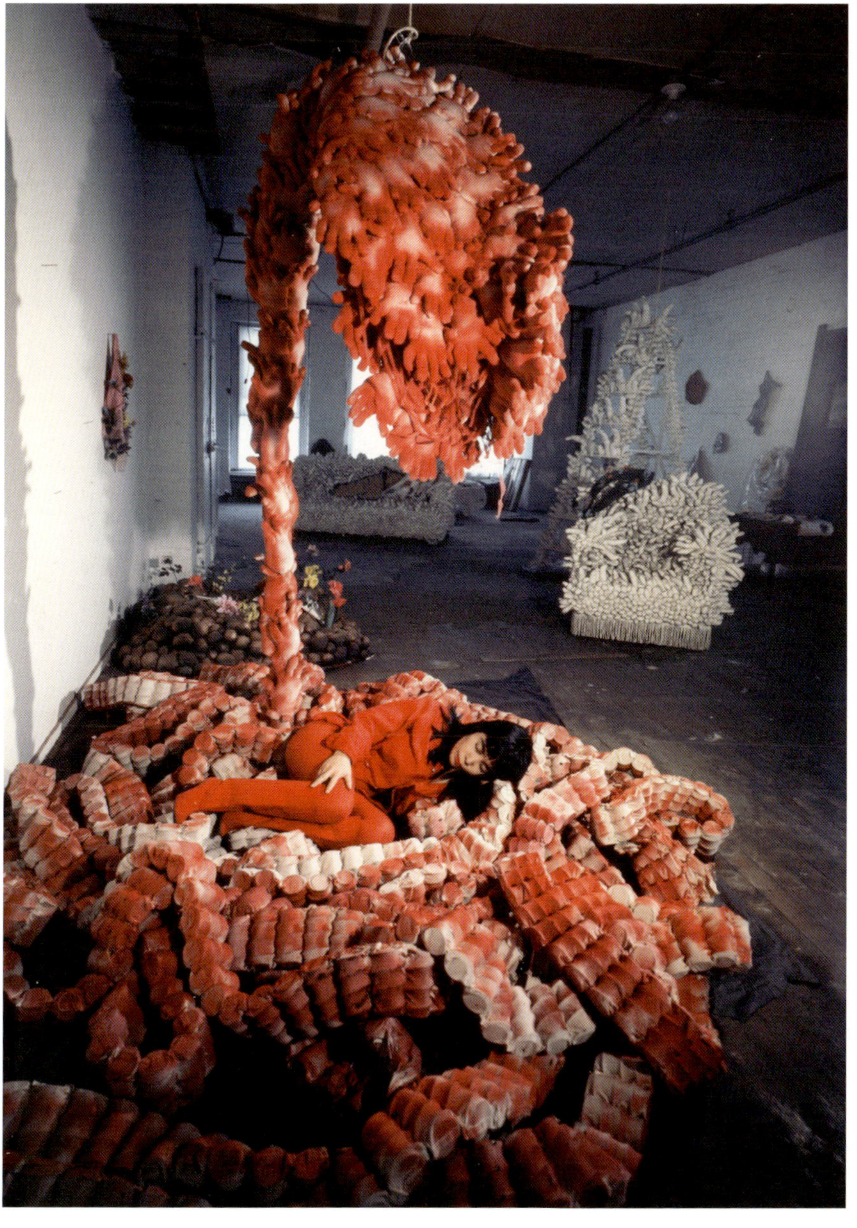

11. Yayoi Kusama lying on *My Flower Bed*
in her studio, New York, 1962

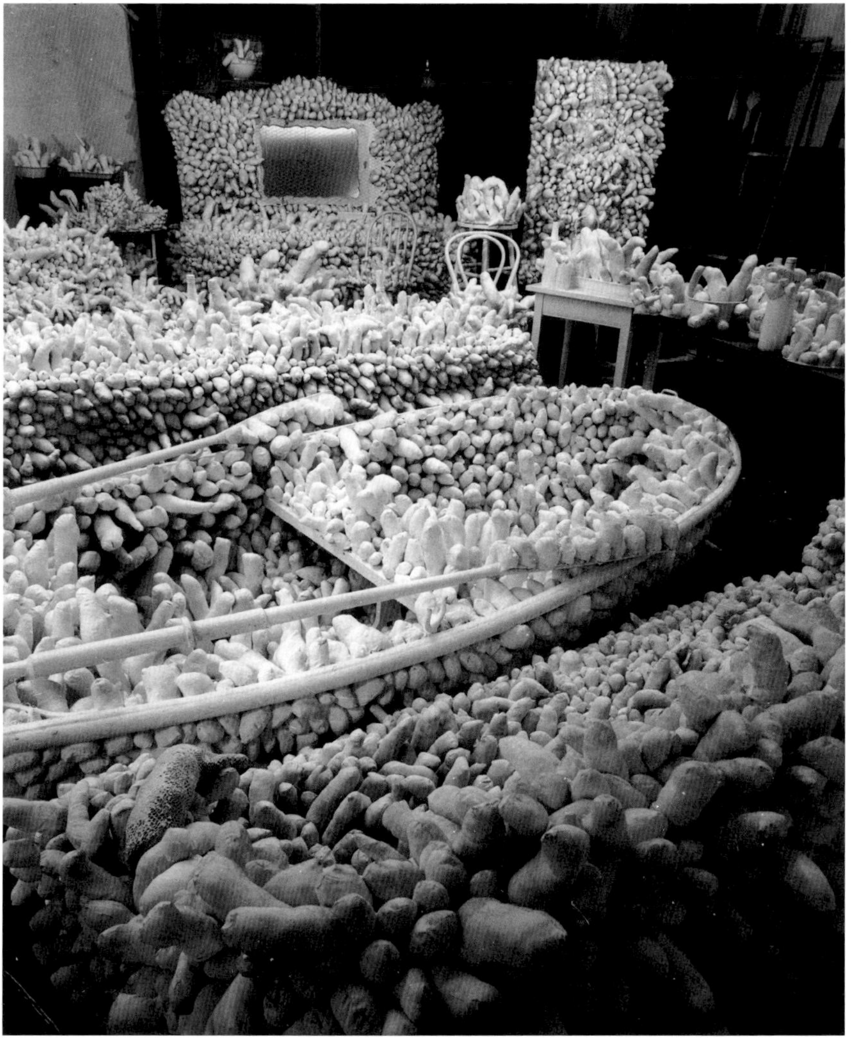

12. Soft sculptures in Kusama's studio,
New York, c.1963

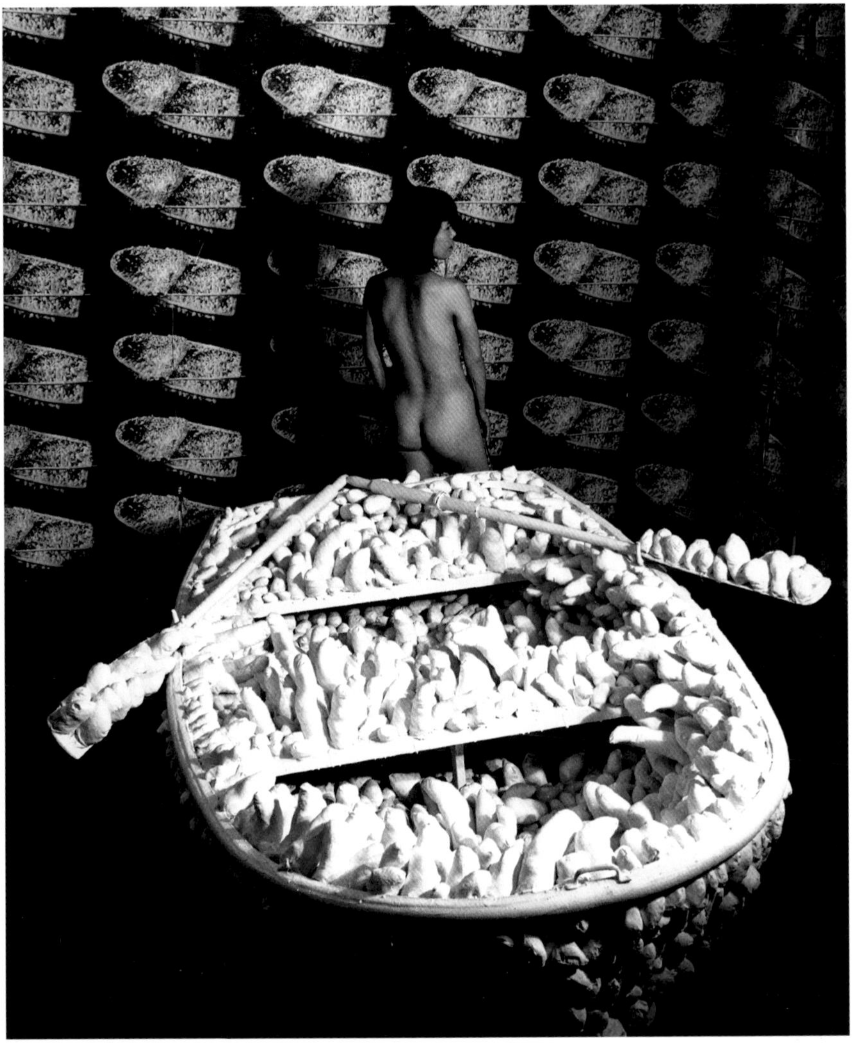

13. Installation view with Yayoi Kusama posing in *Aggregation: One Thousand Boats Show*, Gertrude Stein Gallery, New York, 1963

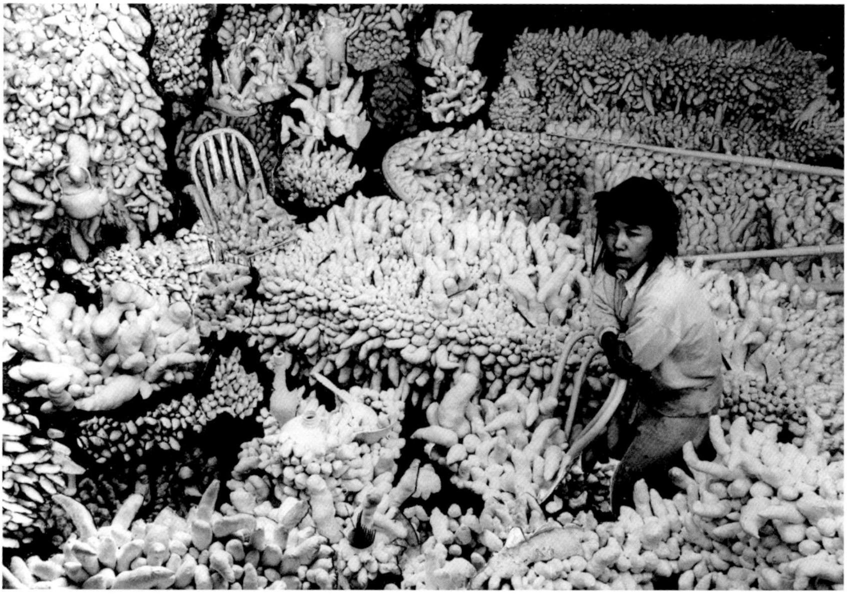

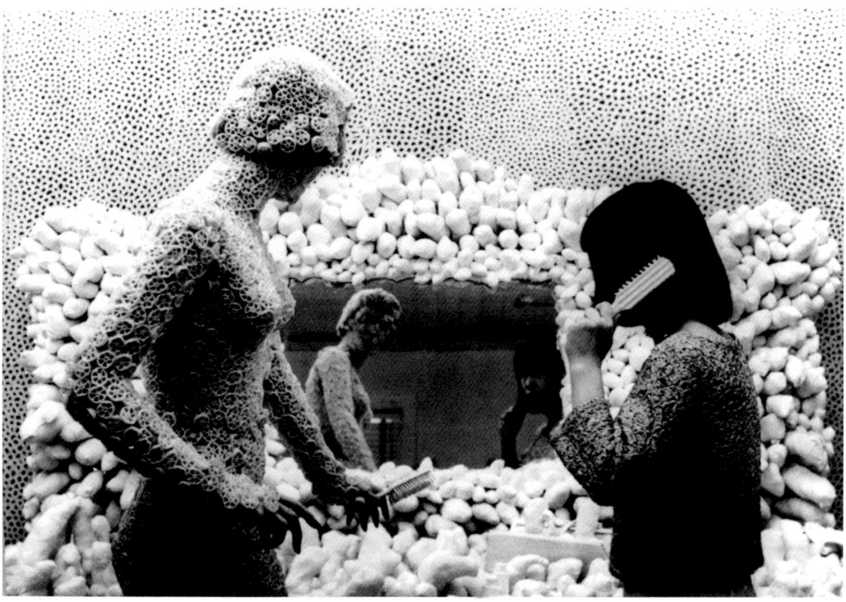

14. Yayoi Kusama,
Compulsion Furniture (Accumulation),
c.1964, photo-collage, 20.3 × 25.1cm

15. Yayoi Kusama in '*Driving Image* Show',
Richard Castellane Gallery, New York,
1964

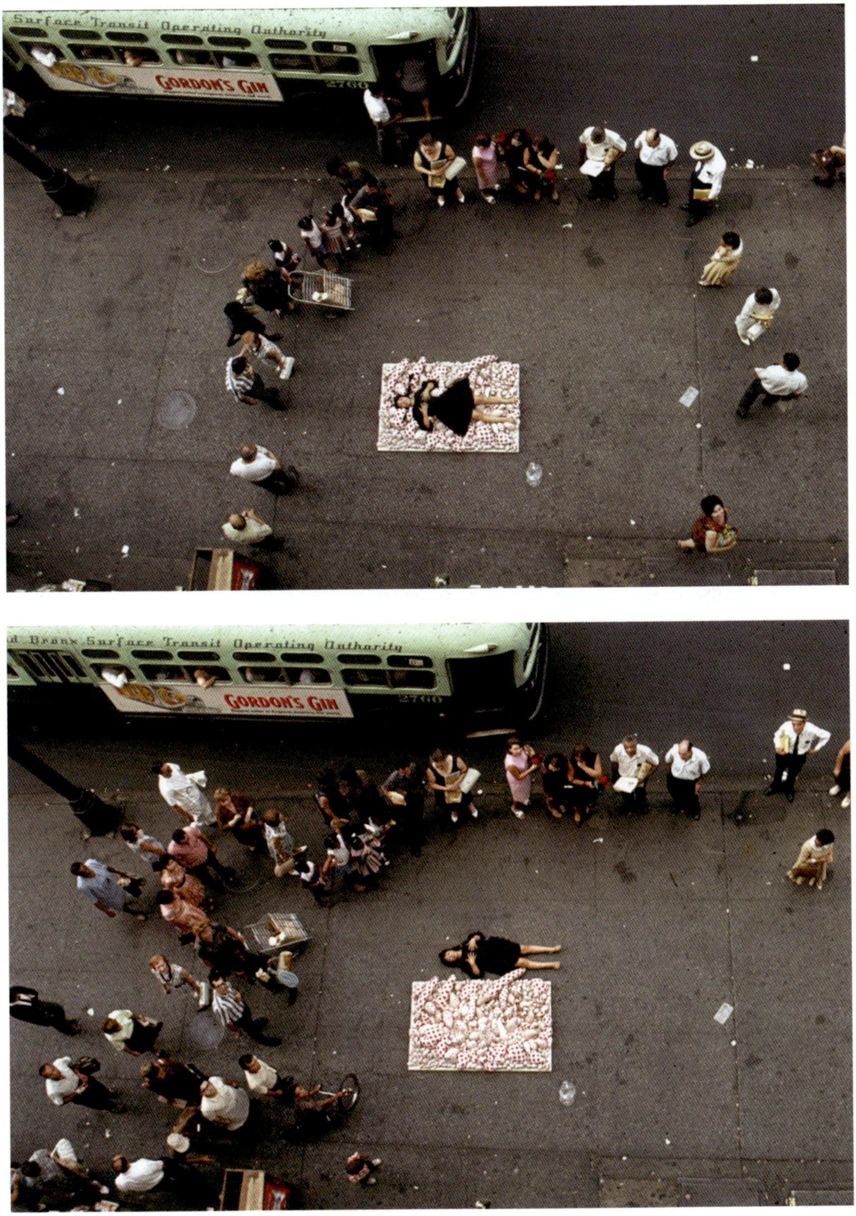

16. Yayoi Kusama,
14th Street Happening, 1966,
New York

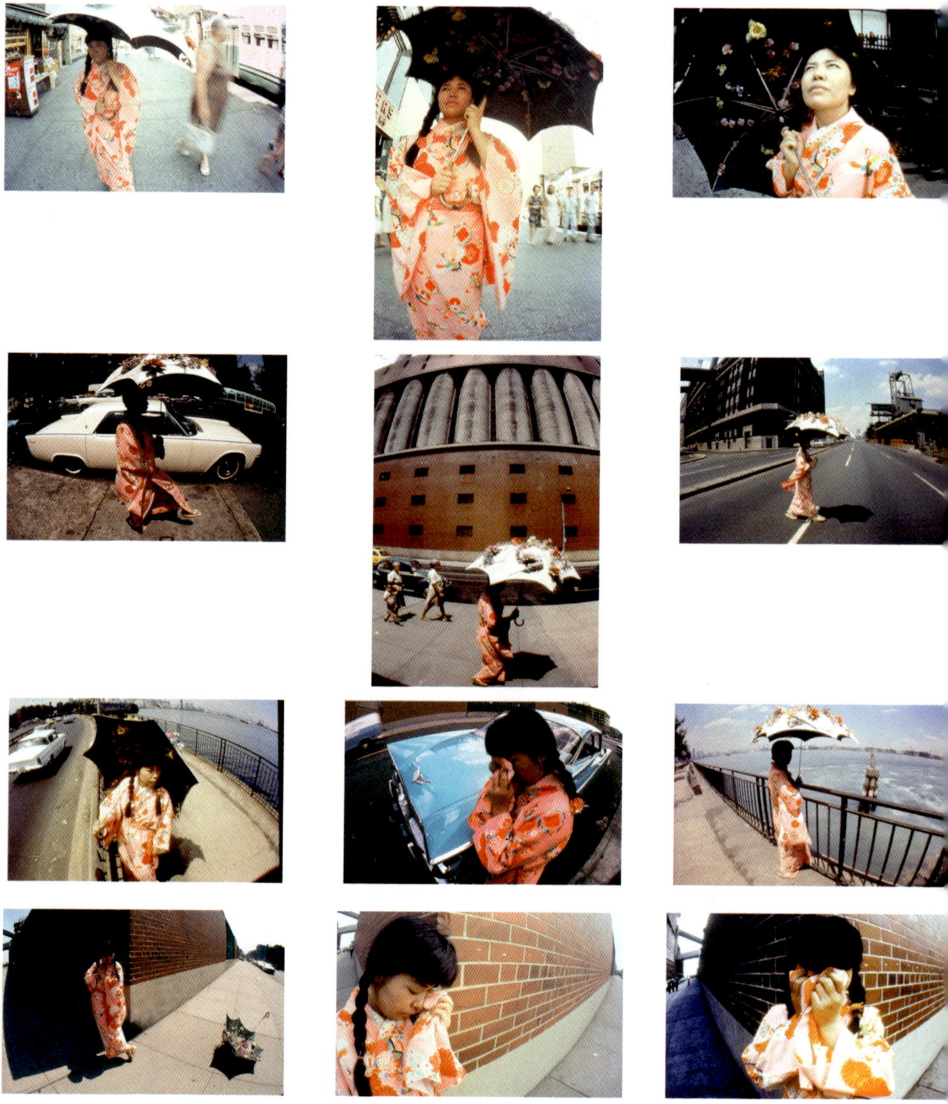

17. Yayoi Kusama,
Walking Piece, 1966,
New York
Photographs: Eikoh Hosoe

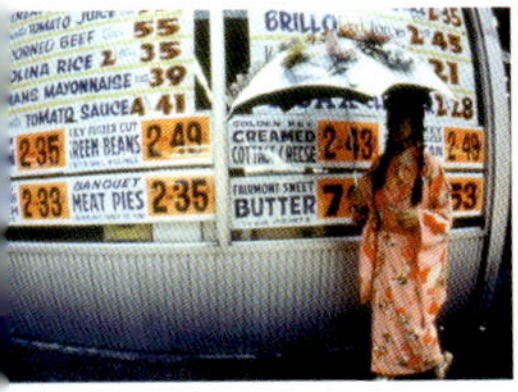

BRILLO
TOMATO SAUCE
GREEN BEANS
CREAMED
MEAT PIES
BUTTER
2·35
2·49
2·33

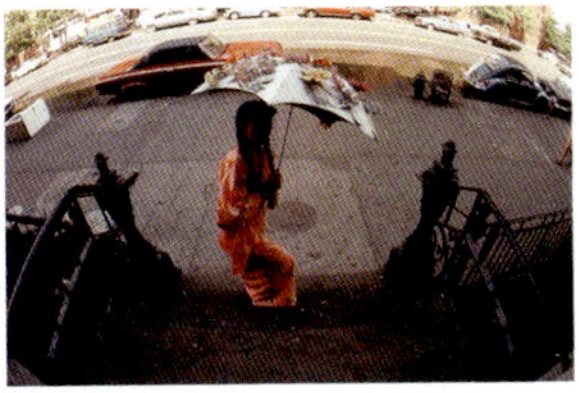

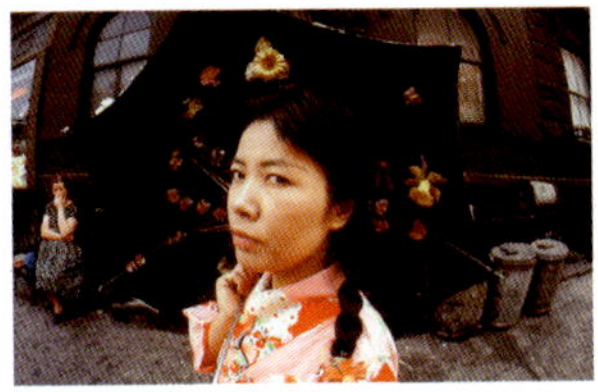

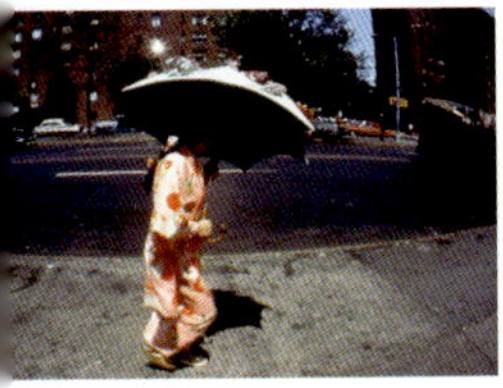

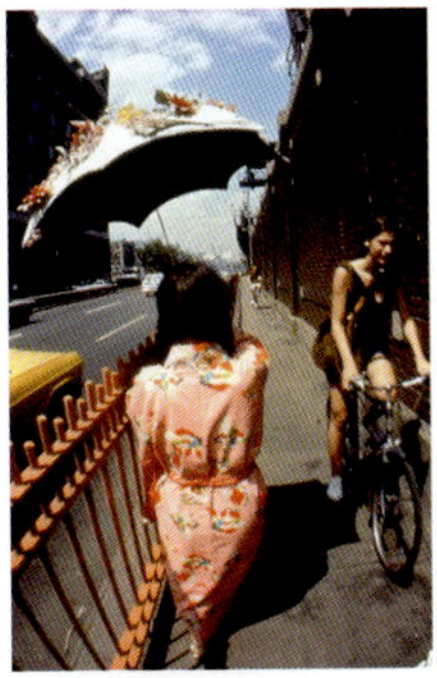

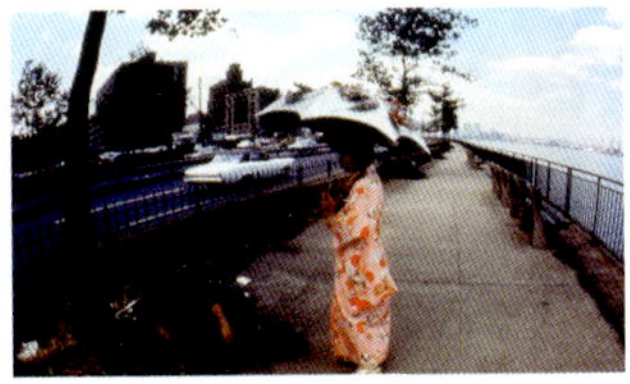

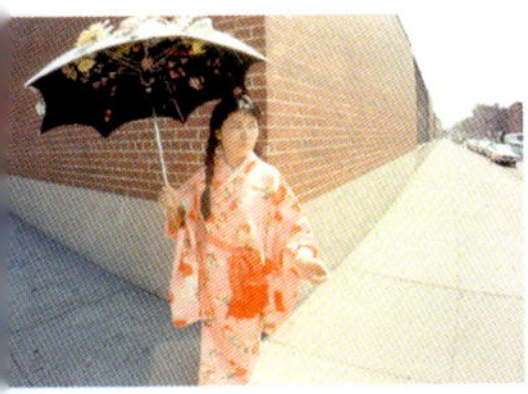

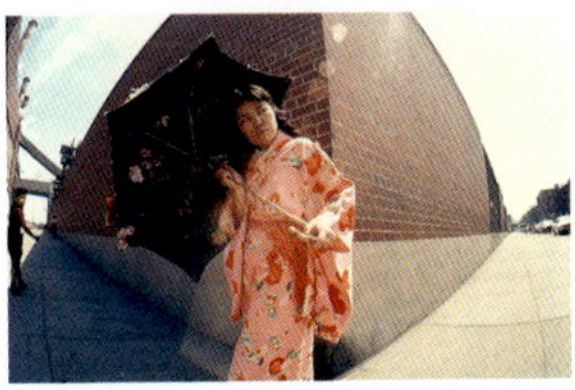

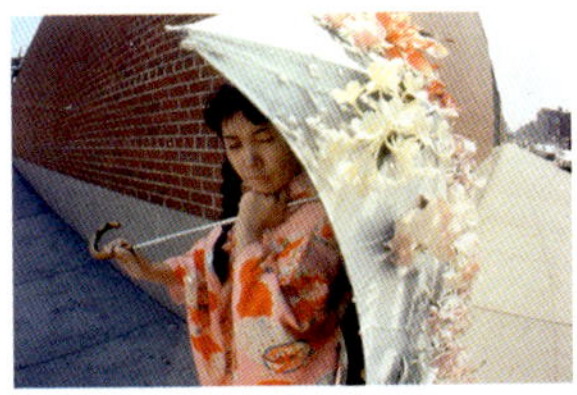

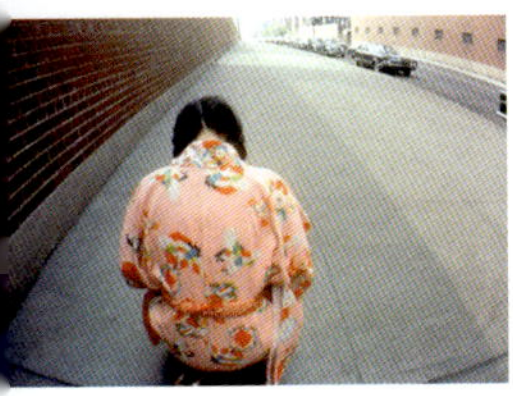

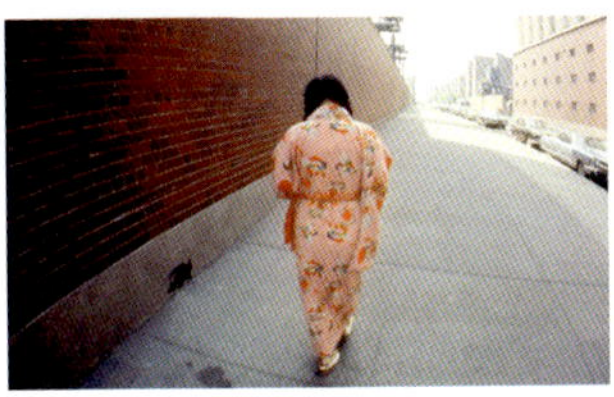

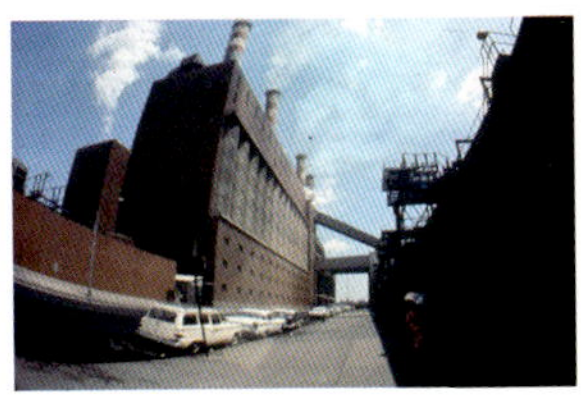

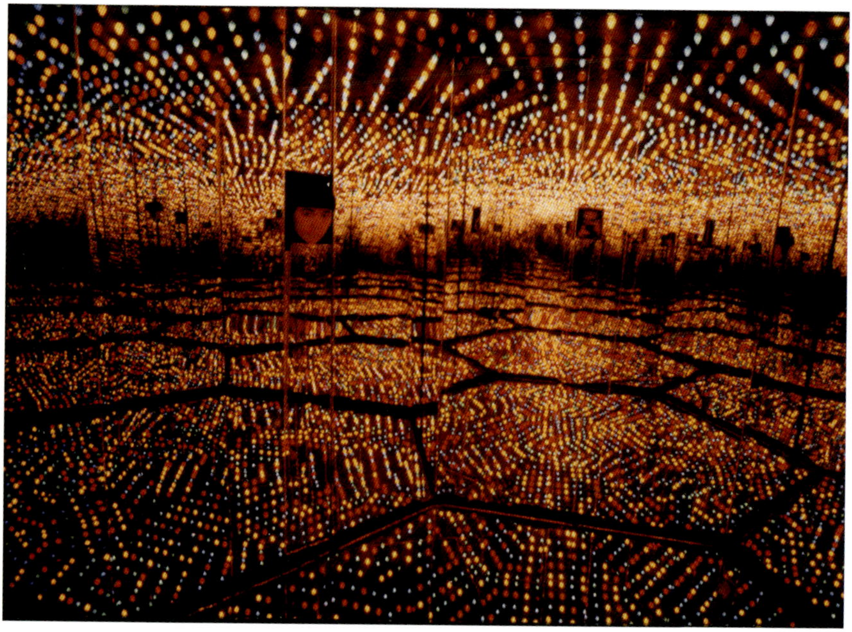

18. Yayoi Kusama,
Kusuma's Peep Show — Endless Love Show, 1966,
mirrors, light bulbs, stainless steel and wood,
approximately 2m wide

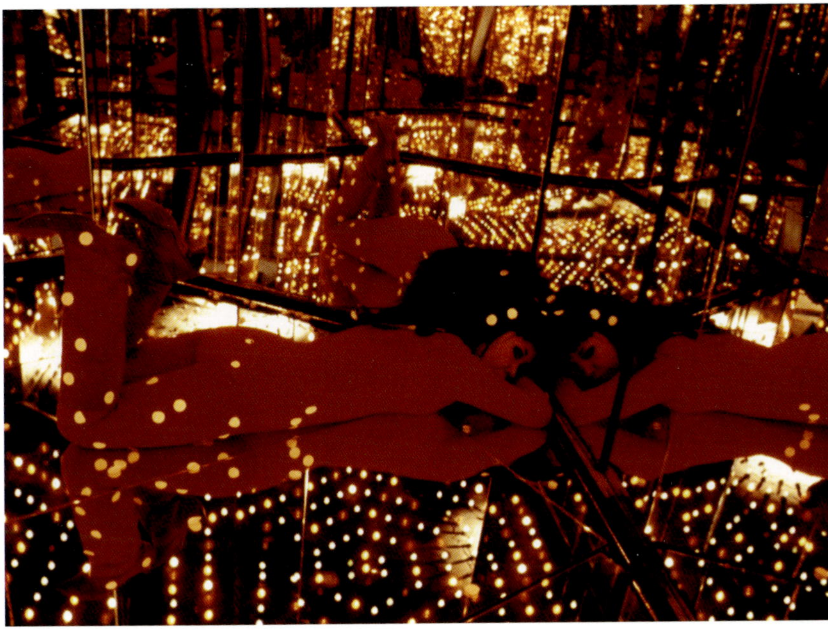

19. Yayoi Kusama inside *Kusama's Peep Show — Endless Love Show*, Richard Castellane Gallery, New York, 1966

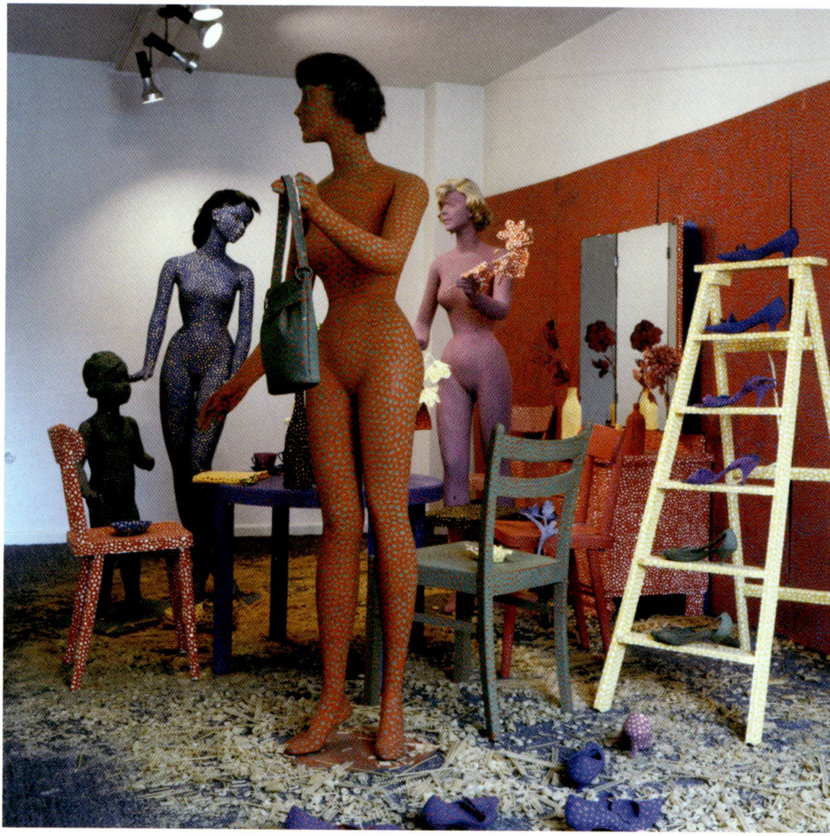

20. Installation view, '*Driving Image* Show', Galerie M.E. Thelen, Essen, Germany, 1966

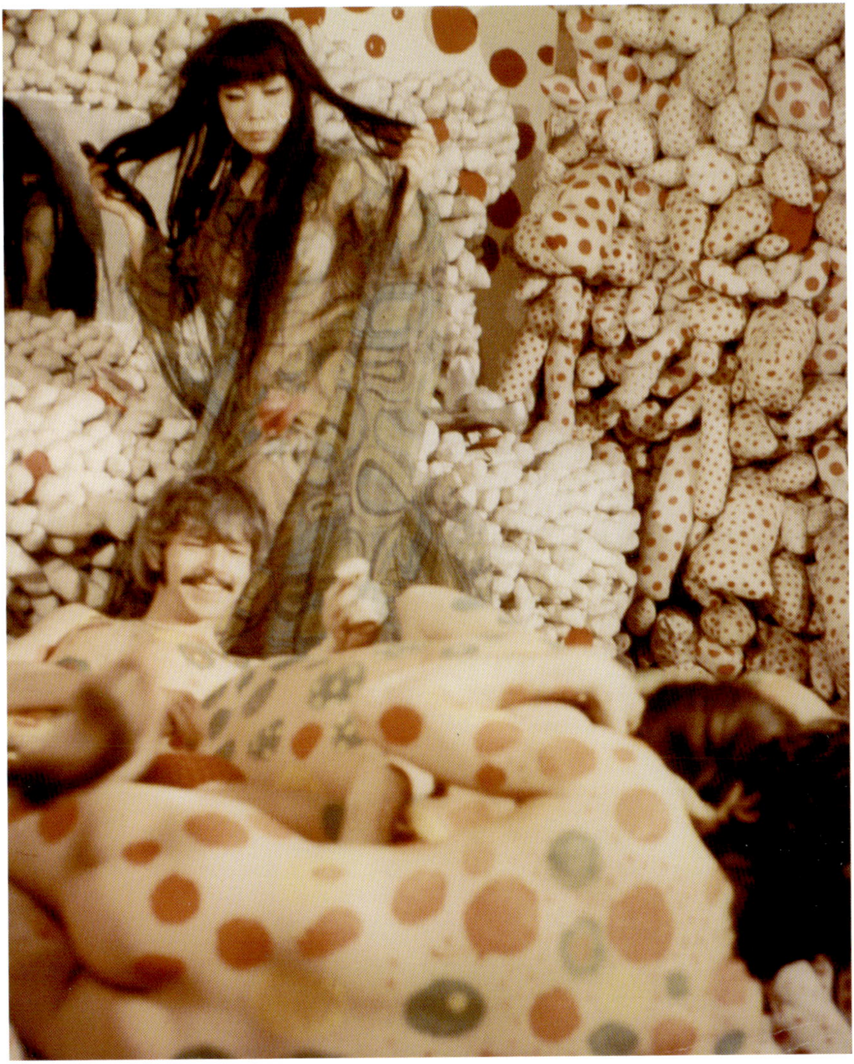

21. Yayoi Kusama,
Homosexual Happening, 1968,
Kusama's studio, New York,
Photograph: Bill Baron

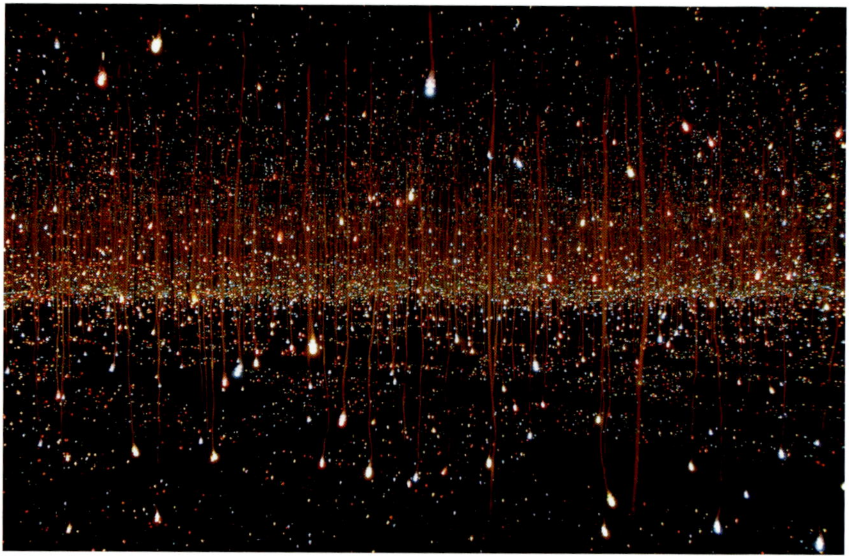

22. Yayoi Kusama,
Fireflies on the Water, 2000,
mirror, plexiglas, light bulbs, metal,
wood and water,
442.4 × 442.4 × 320cm

as decrying the market's financial support of the war in Vietnam, Kusama declared: 'Obliterate Wall Street Men with Polka Dots on Their Naked Bodies!'[91] Her 1968 psychedelic film *Self-Obliteration* includes scenes of painted participants dancing inside her mirrored room environments, offering a more raucous, collective experience of her enclosed spaces than those photographs she had taken of herself inside. This bringing together of groups of people inside rooms is in stark contrast to her earlier *14th Street Happening*, in which Kusama presented herself shipwrecked on a phalli barnacled raft, an atomised alien subject interrupting the flow of New York City's traffic and residents. By the end of the decade, her practice shifted decidedly in the direction of collective actions, as she acted as a master of ceremonies, orchestrating willing participants.

Throughout the 1960s, Kusama played fast and loose with contemporary political events; by the tail end of the decade, her work appeared to many as a series of publicity stunts involving her familiar repertoire of polka dots and nudity, but lacking her earlier seriousness. This led to articles and reviews in a wide range of media, from the contemporary art press to the so-called 'girlie' magazine trade, both locally and abroad. For example, she was featured in the Australian publication *Man*, which titillated viewers with tales of nudity and public orgies organised by 'a pocket-sized, headstrong Japanese professional sculptress and occasional love goddess who hopes to revolutionise New York'.[92] Kusama produced her own issue of a broadsheet titled *Orgy*, which mimicked the language and typography of porn magazines and also their more 'cultural' counterparts, such as *Screw*, in a somewhat unsuccessful bid to claim her own agency in the distribution process. While on the one hand her group happenings were very much of their time in their media-friendly promotion of 'free love', they also echoed the emergent psychological and sociological discourses then celebrating modes of sexuality and eroticism as a way of breaking out of the repressive societal constraints subjects experienced themselves as working and living under.[93] In the passage from representing *Infinity Mirror Room — Phalli's Field* as a private interior world to her promotion of group occupations in the later happenings, an interesting shift occurred that brings to mind the idea of the collective. This shift might be considered to be obliquely tuned in to Herbert Marcuse's contemporary call for the political confrontation of the establishment through the erotic and social liberation of bodies. Carolee Schneeman, whose group performance *Meat Joy* (1964) featured young performers writhing on the floor while raw fish, sausages, wet paint and plastic were thrown onto their bodies, discussed Kusama's happenings in terms of how they were disruptive social forces that were able to 'penetrate the inherited meaning of culture'.[94]

Because of this shift, *Infinity Mirror Room — Phalli's Field* offered an important intervention into the changing nature of the aesthetic experience during the 1960s. A growing number of artists were keen to forge new ways of making art and thinking about it in the aftermath of what seemed to them an exhausted post-War High Modernist model that championed Abstract Expressionism — the 'Action Painting' epitomised in Hans Namuth's photographs of Pollock at work in 1950, flinging and hurling paint across the canvas. Kusama recalls how hard it was for work by newcomers to the avant-garde art scene in New York to 'extricate itself from the spell of Action Painting', which 'was all the rage then [...] everybody was adopting this style and selling the stuff at outrageous prices. My paintings were the polar opposite in terms of intention.'[95] Harold Rosenberg, writing on Abstract Expressionism, made the biggest impact on the new generation of artists, with Allan Kaprow in particular picking up on Rosenberg's characterisation of 'Action Painting' as an 'arena' in which they 'acted'. In his account,

Rosenberg inadvertently provided an alternative trajectory for theorising what would later come to be called the 'participatory' artwork. If by the 1960s the main tenets of the modernist theory underpinning Abstract Expressionism had been largely dismantled by new forms of critical and artistic practice, the idea that large-scale abstract painting might be read as an expanded arena of action or participation remained, capturing the interest of artists (Kusama included) who were keen to establish alternative ways of imagining the spectator's encounter with the work of art as far from purely 'optical' or visual in affect. For what Rosenberg had emphasised was how Pollock's painting was, above all, about a bodily, physical encounter.

Rosenberg described how, in the immediate aftermath of World War II, painting underwent a radical sea change:

> *the canvas began to appear to one American painter after another as an arena in which to act — rather than as a space in which to reproduce [...] What was to go on the canvas was not a picture but an event.*[96]

Through this reading, aspects of the environment in which the painting was made are manifest on the surface of the canvas, and the lived time or duration of its production prominent. As Rosenberg put it,

> *The painter no longer approached his easel with an image in his mind; he went up to it with material in his hand to do something to that other piece of material in front of him. The image would be the result of this encounter.*[97]

For Rosenberg, thinking of the act of painting as precisely that — as an action — had important implications for the status of the artist and also the viewer. Kaprow picked up on Rosenberg's argument about 'action' and his emphasis on the materiality of the painting process in his 1958 essay 'The Legacy of Jackson Pollock', in which he described Pollock's painting as an early example of the artwork as an event that focused on material and experiential aspects, rather than optical and transcendent ones.[98] Kaprow understood Pollock as offering a vividly visceral and fully three-dimensional experience — an important precursor to Kaprow's future happenings. Pollock, Kaprow wrote, 'ignored the confines of the rectangular field in favour of a continuum going in all directions simultaneously, beyond the literal dimensions of any work.'[99]

As Judith Rodenbeck has noted, environments and happenings were, for Kaprow, 'passive and active versions of a radically extended visual practice' that should be understood 'in terms of the turn to process and participation in the arts'.[100] While Kusama, like Kaprow, insisted on the extension of her paintings beyond the 'literal dimensions' of the canvas, it was with her room environments that she offered her most radical reconfiguration of the viewing encounter.

For Kaprow the role of the participant in the happening could not be fully scripted. The only rule was that, unless specifically instructed by whoever produced the 'score' for the happening, all attending subjects must become actively involved in the proceedings. Acknowledging how quickly the cliché of participation had led to a certain kind of apathy among viewers, Kaprow demanded that, however minimal the instructions, all persons involved in a happening be 'willing and committed participants who have a clear idea of what they are to do'.[101] In such environments 'there is no question that one is inside and, for better or worse, a real part of the whole'. The willing participants, he wrote, become 'immersed' in the space.[102] At times, Kaprow notes, participants would be crowded together inside such environments, arranged in 'tight but informal clusters'; his words call to mind those animate-inanimate bunches of phallic tubers clustered together inside *Infinity Mirror Room — Phalli's Field* and Kusama's later *Driving Image* domestic environments.[103] In his 1966 book *Assemblage, Environments & Happenings*, Kaprow offered extensive archival images of the numerous ephemeral happenings and environments that had taken place since the late 1950s. The book also contained his long essay on such work, in which he discusses Kusama's output, relating it to Clarence Schmidt's environments. Several pages of the photo-essay at the beginning of the book are also dedicated to Kusama's environments, under the subheading 'Endless'. This section includes a number of installation shots of the New York version of '*Driving Image* Show',[104] in which Kusama perches on *Accumulation 2* wearing a printed shift dress that appears to be covered with an 'infinity net'. Another page features a photograph of her brushing her hair, looking slightly away as if to echo the affect-free aspect of the plastic mannequin beside her. Despite her wooden appearance, Kusama is a mimetic participant in the scene, mirroring the actions of the inanimate dummy with her own stilled yet vital gestures, placing the question of active participation under pressure (fig.15).

The Gutai group, which included Jiro Yoshihara, Akira Kanayama, Saburo Murakami, Kazuo Shiraga and Shozo Shimamoto, first emerged in Japan in 1954, determined to break free from the stranglehold of European modernism through an expansion of art's boundaries beyond the canvas and into the surrounding environment. This avant-garde movement offered a radical break with previous Japanese art practice, such as the traditional form of Nihonga painting that Kusama had trained in — a practice that had its roots in early twentieth-century expressionism and biomorphic surrealism, and a world apart from the kinds of experimental and time-based works then being conducted by Gutai artists. Producing publications, manifestos and public events and actions, the Gutai artists rapidly gained a reputation in the New York art scene as their activities were reported in the art press.[105] For example, Murakami's performance *Sakuhin (Tsuka)* (*Work/Performance (Break Though)*, 1956), in which he burst through a series of large paper sheets tacked taut against a wooden frame, marking the paper with only the ripped holes caused by his body, deliberately called to mind the hole-studded canvases of Lucio Fontana and the expressive painting gestures of the New York School. Kaprow was quick to recognise this work by Murakami, as well as Shiraga's *Doro Ni Idomu* (*Challenging Mud*, 1955; fig.23), in which the artist was sprawled face down in a mix of mud, gravel and sand, pushing the unctuous thick mess in arm-length sweeps and waves, offering an entirely bodily and environmental reconfiguration of Pollock's 'action painting' — a total immersion in the act of making.[106]

Although Kusama's frequent use of the phrase 'self-obliteration' refers explicitly to her experiences of 'de-personalisation', at several points in her writings and public statements 'self-obliteration' is imbued with positive connotations, alluding to a kind of oceanic bliss in that moment of feeling lost to one's surroundings. This slippage between alternate states is a crucial structural device for Kusama — wrong-footing spectators and introducing a note of ambivalence in their encounter with her work. In fact, one aim of her *Orgy* happenings was to instantiate for her naked participants an experience of 'self-obliteration' to suggest a moment of unity, of coming together and blending with other bodies and the surrounding environment. As she described it, 'The spectators and performers seemed to melt into one, filling the studio with an indescribable sense of rapture.'[107]

Just as Kusama's public happenings from 1968, such as the *Naked Protest at Wall Street*, were presented as overt political critiques and, later, antiwar protests, so *Infinity Mirror Room — Phalli's Field* sought to bring subjects together in an environment structured by play as well as unity — a coming together of people (and polka dots) that was a trademark across her work and served to critique established order. Perhaps one question posed by the environment is what kind of subject emerges when the individual subject is erased. Being told how to act, where to stand and what to do not only rankles, but can positively oppress viewers when they are made active 'participants' by dint of simply being present — precisely the opposite of the kind of experience Kusama and Kaprow sought to produce. Whether an 'active' or 'passive' form of participation is required of the viewer — Kusama's most recent 'obliteration rooms' involve inviting visitors to actually stick coloured polka dots to the walls and surfaces of the interior space themselves — the status of the subject, as 'viewer', 'participant' or 'voyeur' remains unresolved.[108]

Kusama's Free World

In *Walking Piece* (fig.17), a performance work from 1966, Kusama documented herself walking around Manhattan wearing traditional Japanese dress — a pale pink kimono — and carrying a small, decorated parasol that she variously used to hide her face and shield her body. This low-key, one-person happening was subsequently exhibited as a slide show, in which her movements were tracked awkwardly: as the slides clump down into the projector, the fluid movements of Kusama's performance are reduced to a disjointed series of similar yet different images. In one shot she walks past a grocery store with its windows covered in advertisements. In another she stands on a street corner, covering her face with her hands. Passers-by watch her with open interest, and she is seen looking down at a homeless person who sits under a tree on the sidewalk; later it is Kusama who crouches close to the ground with her back to the camera. In each of the photographic slides Kusama's appearance is out of place, reflecting popular orientalist fantasies, as a nomadic out-of-place subject whose traditional clothing and demureness are jarring against the urban New York setting. Outside the confines of the endless interior of *Infinity Mirror Room — Phalli's Field*, the artist no longer embodies the sex-kitten pin-up conveying a certain mode of mastery over her environment, but rather is the 'foreign' subject who performs a 'dislocation' that is geographic and cultural, not phenomenological or psychological. The question of 'freedom' that was posed by the subject's experience in the closed mirrored environments and wrangled with by Gilman's trapped protagonist is here reframed around a mode of encounter in which difference and repetition operate according to another register. *Walking Piece* speaks to the global as well as local environments that subjects inhabit, casting a new inflection on Kusama's clarion call to 'Become part of your environment'.[109]

Despite the overtly political sloganeering of many of Kusama's later happenings, from *Homosexual Happening* to *Naked Protest at Wall Street* to anti-Vietnam War protests in 1968, Kusama has always resisted explicit affiliation with any political movement. However, her entire career can be read as a response to both social and psycological conflict.[110] Kusama grew up in the shadow of World War II, and the years she spent in New York were characterised by the hardships of city dwelling. By the late 1960s her responses to such difficulties found voice in the series of happenings she staged in New York. The reason the more serious and political aspect of her work tends to be neglected is that, as Mignon Nixon has noted, 'Kusama does not behave like a "political" artist' — she has no clear, explicit agenda, and her frequent outbursts and public declarations in the 1960s were,

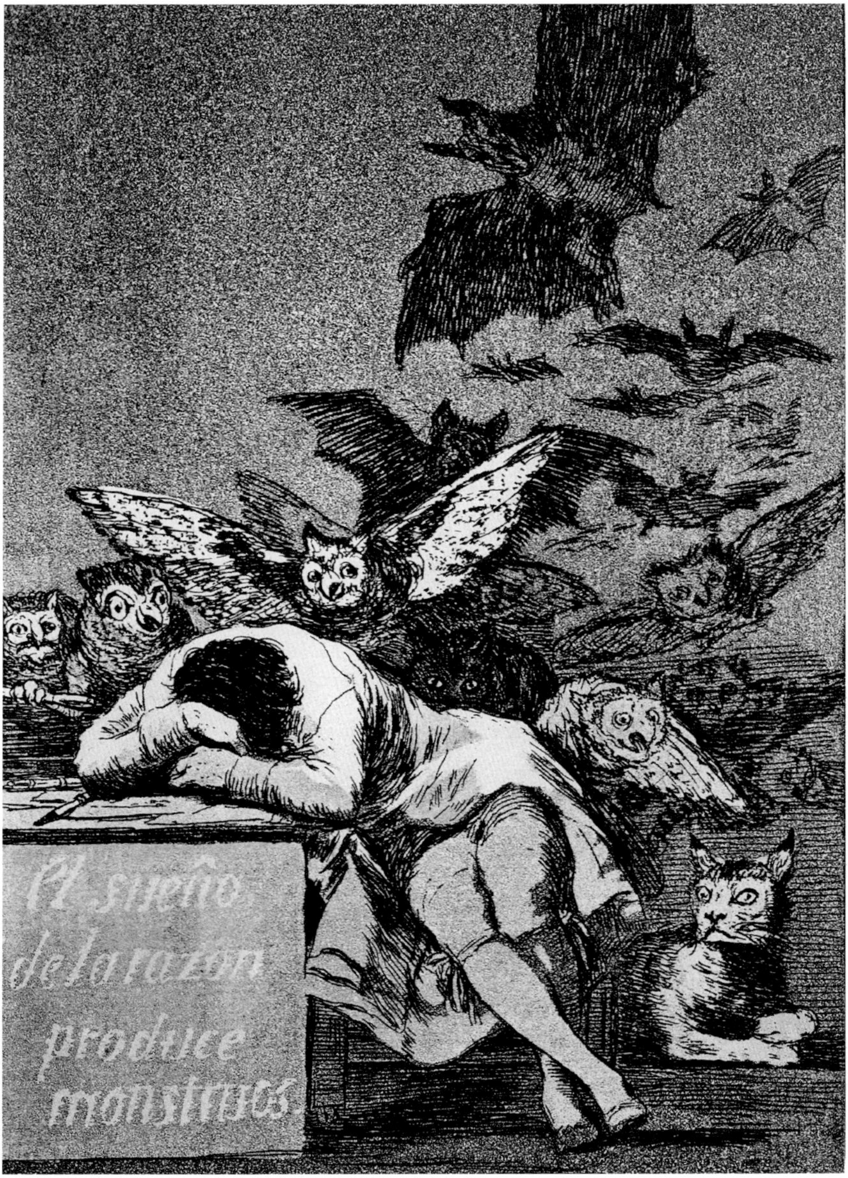

23. Francisco José de Goya,
El sueño de la razón produce monstruos
(*The Sleep of Reason Brings Forth Monsters*),
1796—99, from *Los caprichos*, plate 43,
etching and aquatint, 19 × 13cm

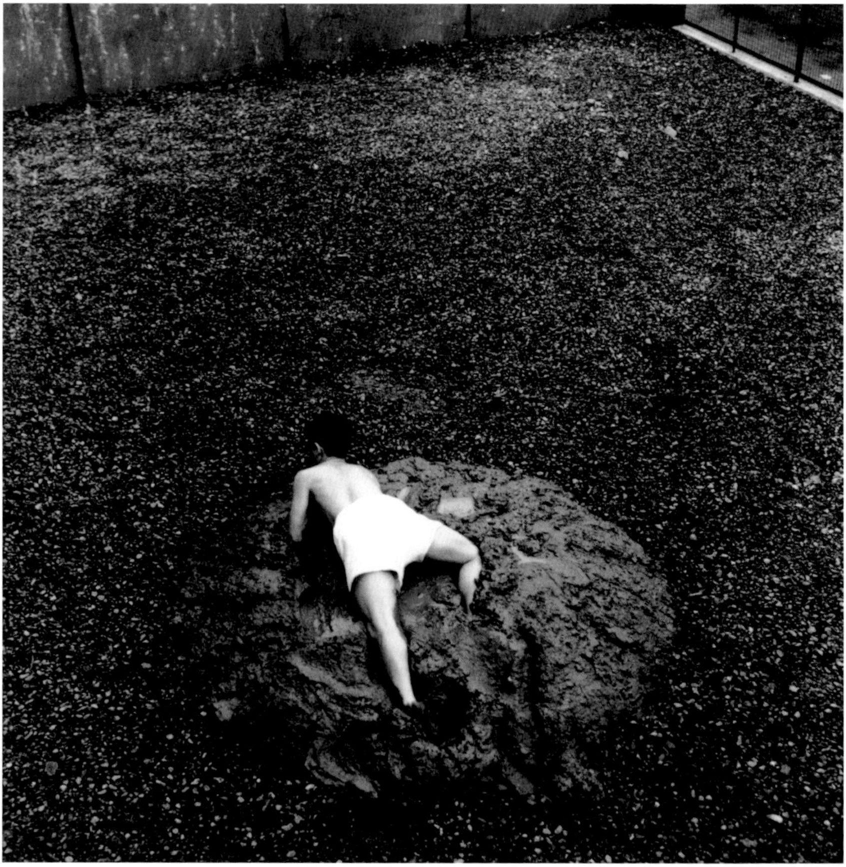

24. Kazuo Shiraga,
Doro Ni Idomu (Challenging Mud), 1955,

Courtesy Museum of Osaka University

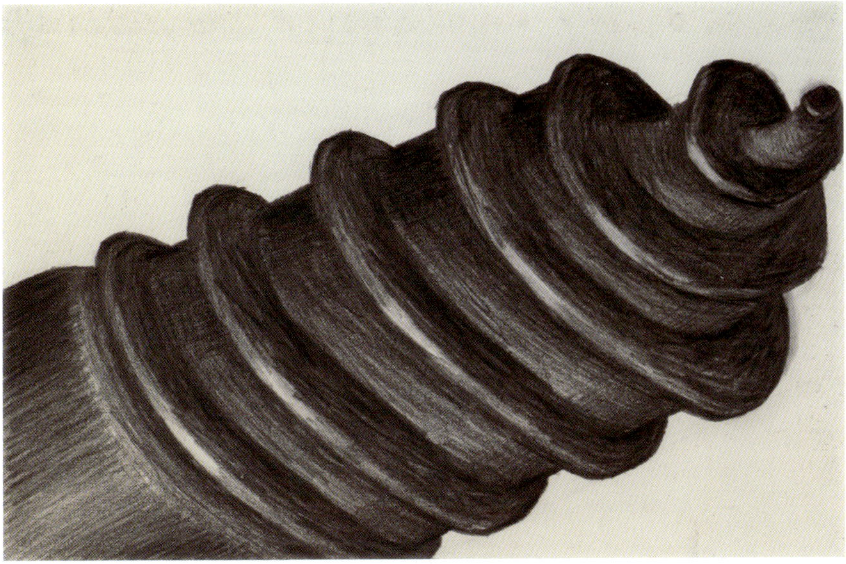

25. Lee Lozano,
No Title, 1964,
graphite on paper,
21 × 32.4cm

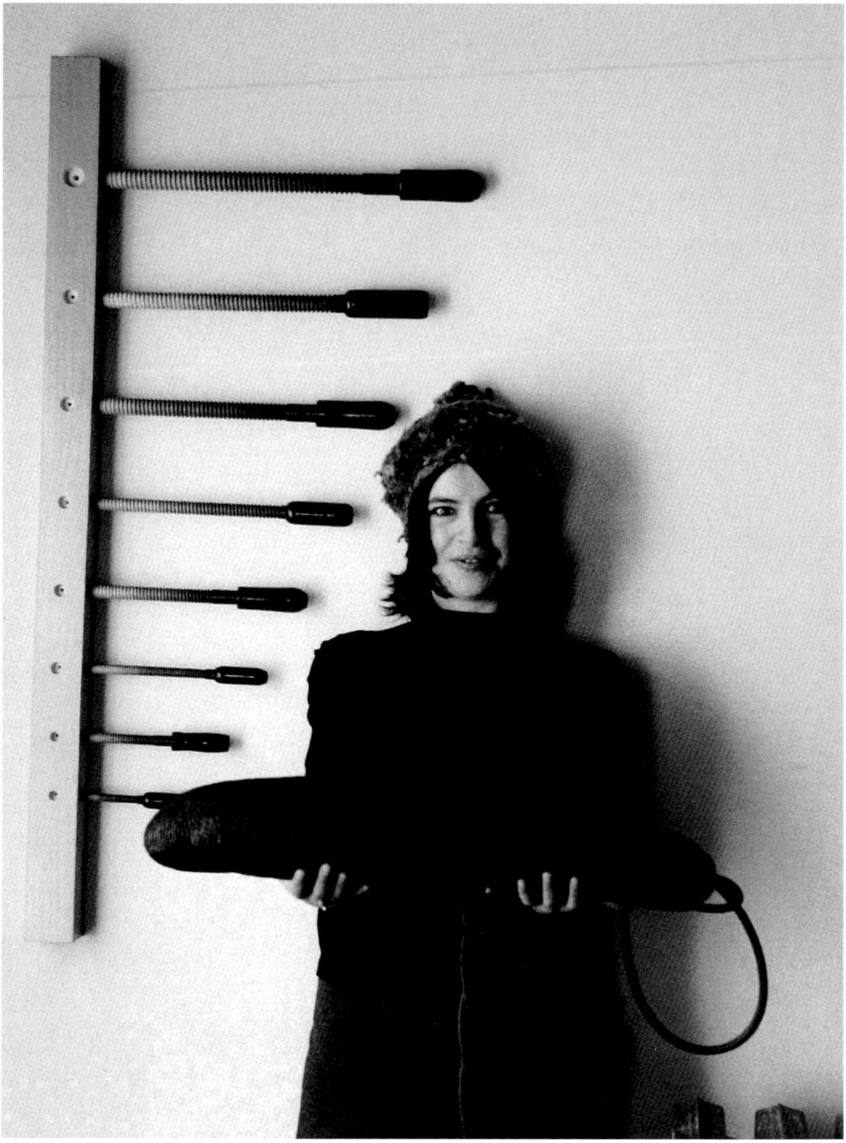

26. Eva Hesse holding *Ingeminate*, 1965
© The Estate of Eva Hesse
Courtesy Münchner Stadtmuseum Collection
Photography, Munich
Photograph: Herman Landshoff

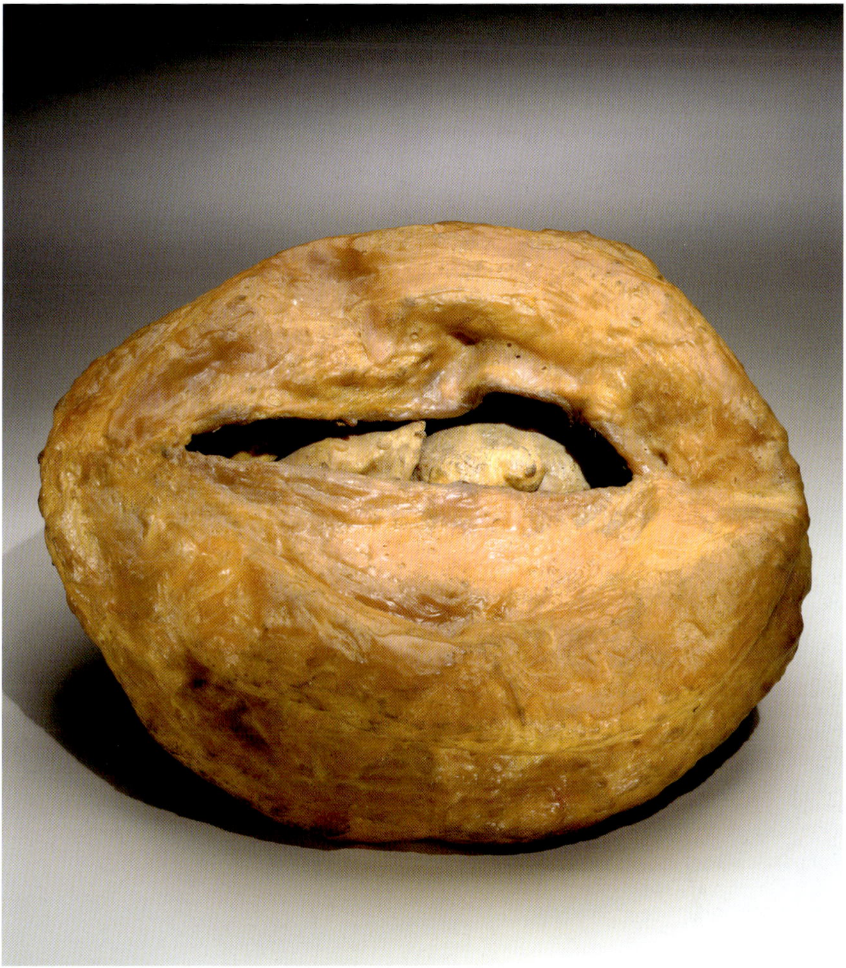

27. Louise Bourgeois,
Le Regard (*The Gaze*), 1966,
latex and cloth,
12.7 × 39.3 × 36.8cm

Courtesy The Easton Foundation
Photograph: Christopher Burke

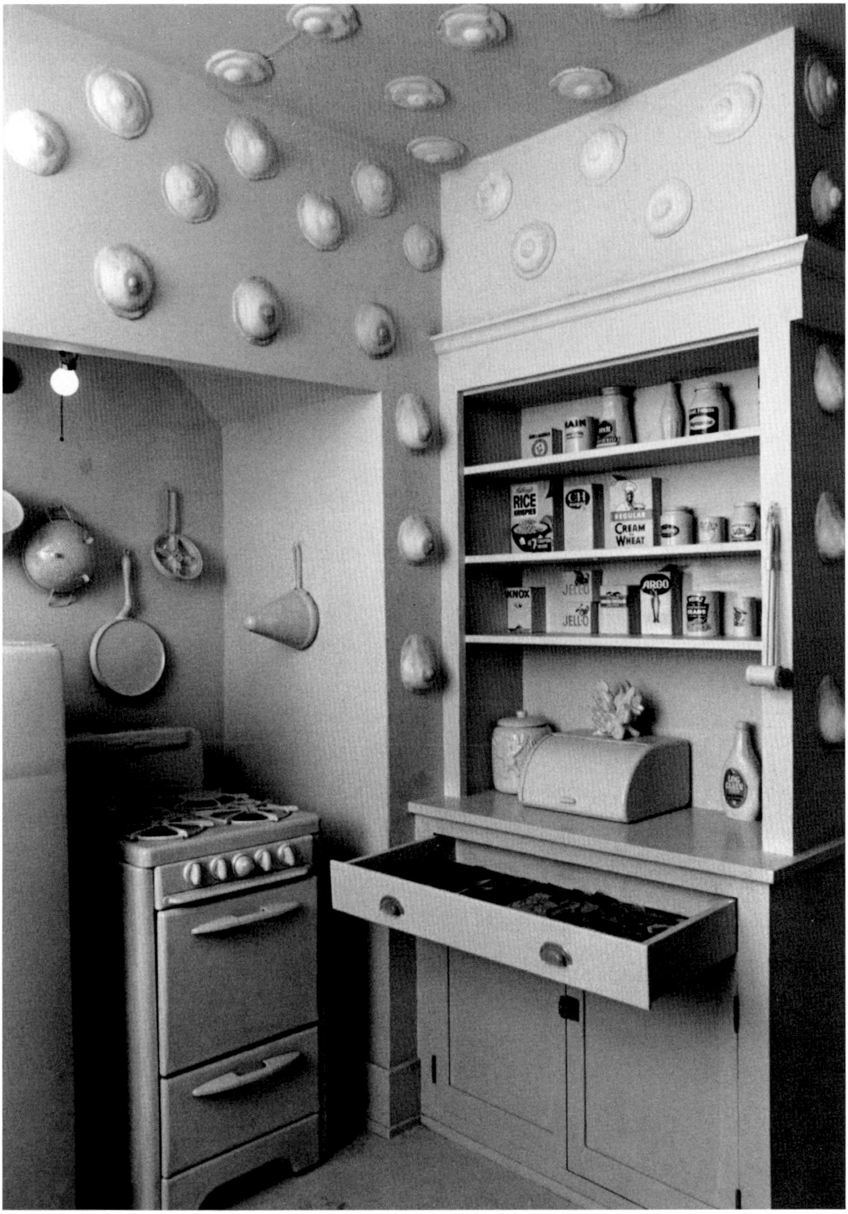

28. Installation view of *Eggs to Breasts* by Vicki Hodgetts in *Nurturant Kitchen* by Susan Frazier, Vicki Hodgetts and Robin Weltsch, 'Womanhouse', Los Angeles, 1972
Courtesy the artists and The Getty Research Institute, Los Angeles
Photograph: Lloyd Hamrol

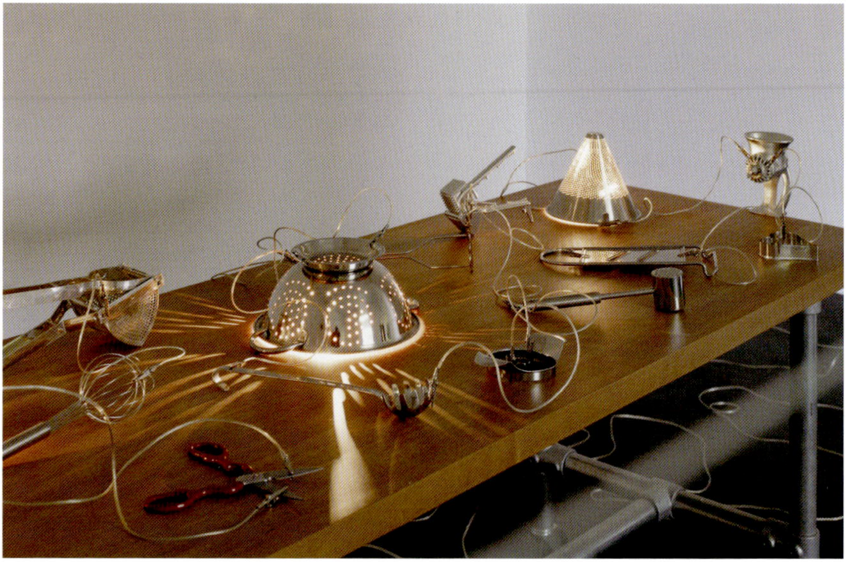

29. Mona Hatoum,
Home, 1999,
wood, stainless steel, electric wire,
computerised dimmer unit,
amplifier and two speakers,
dimensions variable
Photograph: Jörg von Bruchhausen
Courtesy Max Hetzler, Berlin and
White Cube, London

while coruscating, somewhat scattershot in their attack on US international policy.[111] This is not the same, however, as saying that she was apolitical, nor that her overt statements were the only way in which her politics were made apparent.

Kusama's 're-enchantment' of the world, to borrow Félix Guattari's description of her work, offers a vision in which the excesses of a post-War consumer society — the vast process of accumulation of goods in the aftermath of the war in order to protect the future in the face of atomic threat — should be read as both a critical comment and a pathological response.[112] 'I am always deeply interested in the relationship of people and society', Kusama stated in 1964. 'My artistic expressions always grow from the aggregation of these.'[113] As early as 1963, she was alluding, in typically elliptical manner, to her use of repetitive motifs — phallic forms, polka dots and looping webs — as akin to crowds of individual subjects clustered together. 'Polka dots can't stay alone,' she told one interviewer, before likening them to the 'the communicative life of people', in which 'two or three and more polka dots become movement'.[114] When we 'obliterate nature and our bodies with polka dots', she concluded, 'we become part of the unity of our environments'.[115] Kusama here offers an image of her objects as allegories for social relations — an oblique yet compelling model for how she maps her interior environments onto the exterior world. While works such as *Walking Piece* stage this 'unity' with the environment via literal means, this dialectic is seen most spectacularly — and playfully — at work in the interior of *Infinity Mirror Room — Phalli's Field*.

From her early abstract *Infinity Net* paintings to the sculptural objects and room environments that she still produces today, Kusama's artistic project has been characterised by 'an attempt to create a world'.[116] As Judd wrote in his review of the *Infinity*

Net paintings, when viewed up close, the 'small, dense arcs' with which Kusama carefully covered the entire canvas combine to set up a series of 'relationships' that are particularly 'subtle'.[117] For Judd, these designs 'depend on the surrounding area' in a manner akin to the 'infinite' lateral spread of the spotted phallic tubers.[118] Judd used these words to emphasise the cohesiveness of Kusama's work rather than evoking a series of disparate markings. His description can also be used to illustrate the relationships that were established amongst the clusters of phallic bulges, the endless fields of polka dots and the viewers who encounter them or are located among them. Udo Kultermann also identified the 'total ensemble' as the salient feature of Kusama's environments, in which the 'unifying patterned surface' displaces attention from the 'individual work' to the overall experience of the crowded room.[119]

Infinity Mirror Room — Phalli's Field is a precariously structured space in which a model of inclusion and participation rather than atomisation and singularity is tentatively promoted as a viable alternative. 'Let's get to know one another,' Kusama declared in the announcement for her 1968 happening *Take a Subway Ride from Jail to Paradise*.[120] According to the press release, the event was due to take place inside another small enclosed interior — in this instance a subway carriage — reflecting Kusama's ambivalent relationship to containment and a dialectic between captivity and utopian freedom in her work. Kusama has always included elements in her installations that create strange relational habits and effects. In such discombobulating scenarios, the subject is placed under scrutiny by the mirrored walls, while the spotted forms encroach on their previously privileged status and physical location 'outside' or adjacent to the work of art. In Kusama's recasting of that encounter in *Infinity Mirror Room — Phalli's Field*, no such distance or demarcation between subject and object is made possible. On the contrary, Kusama produces an environment — a *world* — in which one is always aware of the other inhabitants of the room, whether they be inanimate spotty stalagmites, other human bodies or one's own mirrored reflection. In her work, subjects are brought together in an 'arena', to borrow Rosenberg's term, where they are provided the space and means to act and take part.

For her 1960 essay 'Freedom and Politics: A Lecture', Hannah Arendt wrote that 'The *raison d'être* of politics is freedom, and its field of experience is action'.[121] Arendt had already outlined this claim in her 1958 book *The Human Condition*, in which she argued that in order for an act to be deemed political, it must occur in a public arena — a 'space of appearances'.[122] In other words, it is not enough that one does something; for it to be political, and therefore to qualify as action, it must be done in front of one's peers. In Arendt's model, politics takes place within the relationships established among participating or 'acting' subjects.[123] With this in mind, Kusama's demand for collective participation, powerfully articulated in her 1968 rallying cry 'Let's get to know one another', is striking — less as an instance of publicity-seeking at a time when she was embracing the free love and happenings movements, than as a potentially radical mode of what Arendt called 'world-building'.[124] *Infinity Mirror Room — Phalli's Field* offers an example of such an attempt at 'world-building', as do the nets of her earlier paintings. The mirror room creates an environment in which subjects might come together in a manner that has implications beyond the private experience of the individual, including her psychological states, addressing instead the wider field of what it is to encounter the world in all its pluralities and multiple modes of being, experiencing, acting and speaking. But it reminds us too of the fragility of that position, of its potential failure as a model of world-building, and the possibility that it might resist such utopian promise — think of those images of Kusama, alone, inside the room.

As Johanna Drucker has argued, the happening is 'most distinctly defined *as relations among individuals*'.[125] Just as Kusama's work tends to be exhibited most successfully when clustered, so, too, it is hard to see one of her net paintings without calling to mind, say, the phallic-studded boat, or perhaps a polka-dotted carpet — they fold and morph into one another as if part of one continuous stream of dots and spots, soft forms and bodies. In her recent room installations, such as *Fireflies on the Water* (2000; fig.22), Kusama has worked hard to blur boundaries between subjects and objects, in breathtaking darkened mirror rooms lit only by pulsating displays of hanging lights. As the lights are reflected across the walls, ceiling and shallow pools of water, the work echoes the earlier panels of spotted phallic forms in *Infinity Mirror Room — Phalli's Field*, through which crowds of viewers wandered. In her dazzling mirrored infinity rooms, Kusama offers a more joyful — because fantastical — experience, something her earlier installations such as *Infinity Mirror Room — Phalli's Field* never quite achieved. The spectacular effects of Kusama's recent rooms replace the more complicated dialectical position upon which the earlier rooms necessarily rely. The physical environment of *Infinity Mirror Room — Phalli's Field* never dissolved entirely, just as the fabric spotted tubers didn't simply register as an 'infinite wonderland': viewers remained aware at all times of the material conditions under which the work had been produced and within which they found themselves. *Infinity Mirror Room — Phalli's Field* was not a world apart, it was not the ephemeral or heady fantasy of blissful immateriality that the later mirror rooms have sought to generate. Instead it was a 'potential space' in which viewers, as subjects, experimented with new modes of being and living. Far from suggesting this is a magical or purely psychic space,

Kusama reminds us that such experiences are part and parcel of our everyday reality. In describing the kind of effect her work should have, she has invoked not just the psychological but also the environmental — that is, those social relations she has sought to understand:

> *Psychological and physical frictions abound in the rifts between human beings and the enigmatic, civilised jungle they inhabit. I am deeply interested in trying to understand the relationships between people, society and nature; and my work is forged from accumulations of these frictions.*[126]

'Friction' is a helpful term to consider in thinking about the affective responses Kusama's work produces. *Infinity Mirror Room — Phalli's Field* was a world in which conflicting webs of relationships were generated and resolved, invoked playfully and mapped spatially. No single grand gesture, political agenda or ideological framework structured the work. There was a deliberate open-endedness to the room — it presented visitors with a 'space of appearances', in which each subject's actions challenged and shaped the contours of the experience. *Infinity Mirror Room — Phalli's Field* attempted to produce a push and pull between conflicting modes of encounter — between the psychological situation in which one's sense of self is fractured and multiplied, and a utopian sense of liberation, playfulness and possibly plenitude. It provided a 'potential space' that was at turns unsettling and emancipating, erotic and psychotic, playful and deadly serious. Above all, *Infinity Mirror Room — Phalli's Field* articulated the transformation of the possibilities of the artwork in the 1960s, as it turned from a discrete, closed form — what Judd would dub in another context the 'specific object' — to an open, expanded and fundamentally experiential environment.[127] It paved the way for the Land art movement of the late 1960s, which saw artists such as Mary Miss and Robert

Smithson working at a large expansive scale outside of the gallery. It also opened up the field for contemporary participatory art practices that insist on the active involvement of viewers in producing an 'open work'; take, for example, Rirkrit Tiravanija, whose early works have involved providing visitors with food and encouraging them to mingle, or Thomas Hirschhorn, whose large installation-cum-library spaces are installed in communities outside the usual 'art world' and used and managed by local residents. Such artists set out to establish a mode of encounter that turns on the question of the social and the communal.

I don't want to overstate the politics of *Infinity Mirror Room — Phalli's Field*, nor do I want it to remain solely within the register of the 'psychological', as if the work existed solely as an idiosyncratic model of Kusama's interior mindscape. On the contrary, it is the fraught relationship between those two registers — the socially engaged and the fractured and atomised, the personal and private and the public and political — that structures our response to this artwork in the most productive and long-lasting way. *Infinity Mirror Room — Phalli's Field* offers both a respite from and a continuation of the kinds of precarious encounters subjects experience in the world 'outside' — captured inside this small mirrored environment, through and through 'Kusama's World'.

1
D.W. Winnicott, 'Playing: A Theoretical Statement', *Playing and Reality*, London: Routledge, 1971, p.51.

2
Infinity Mirror Room — Phalli's Field was initially meant to take place at the Gertrude Stein Gallery, New York, in 1964. Castellane organised two more important exhibitions of Kusama's work between 1965 and 1966. For a detailed biography and exhibition history, see Bhupindra Karia (ed.), *Yayoi Kusama: A Retrospective* (exh. cat.), New York: Center for International Contemporary Art, 1990, p.84. On Kusama's career in New York, see also Midori Yoshimoto, *Into Performance: Japanese Women Artists in New York*, New Brunswick: Rutgers University Press, 2005, pp.45—79.

3
Yayoi Kusama, *Infinity Net: The Autobiography of Yayoi Kusama* (trans. Ralph McCarthy), London: Tate Publishing, 2011, p.51. See also her autobiographical novel *Manhattan Suicide Addict*, Dijon: Les presses du réel, 2005.

4
See J. Laplanche and J.-B. Pontalis, 'Part-Object', *The Language Of Psycho-Analysis*, (1967, trans. Donald Nicholson Smith), London: Karnac Books, 1988, pp.301—02.

5
Y. Kusama, *Infinity Net*, *op. cit.*, p.151.

6
Ibid.

7
Y. Kusama, 'Thoughts on the Mausoleum of Modern Art', press release for the happening *Grand Orgy to Awaken the Dead at MoMA — Featuring Their Usual Display of Nudes*, Rockefeller Gardens, Museum of Modern Art, New York, 25 August 1969; reprinted in Laura Hoptman, 'Yayoi Kusama: A Reckoning', in L. Hoptman et al., *Yayoi Kusama*, London: Phaidon Press, 2000, p.117.

8
Alexandra Munroe, 'Obsession, Fantasy and Outrage: The Art of Yayoi Kusama', in B. Karia (ed.), *Yayoi Kusama: A Retrospective*, *op. cit.*, p.26.

9
On Kusama's *mise en abyme*, see Judith Rodenbeck, 'Yayoi Kusama: Surface, Stitch, Skin', in Catherine de Zegher (ed.), *Inside the Visible: An Elliptical Traverse of 20th Century Art in, of, and from the Feminine* (exh. cat.), Cambridge, MA and London: The MIT Press, 1996, p.151.

10
Y. Kusama, 'A Process to Creation', in Tohru Matsumoto et al., *Yayoi Kusama: Eternity-Modernity* (exh. cat.), Tokyo: National Museum of Art, 2004; as cited in Juliet Mitchell, 'Portrait of the Artist as a Young Flower', in Frances Morris (ed.), *Yayoi Kusama* (exh. cat.), London: Tate Publishing, 2011, p.192.

11
Kusama frequently refers to her work as 'worlds'. See, for example, her interview with Glenn Scott Wright in *Yayoi Kusama, London* (exh. cat.), London: Victoria Miro, 2008, unpaginated. I borrow the term 'open work' from Umberto Eco's book of the same title, in which he argues for the necessarily open-ended relationship that exists between the reader and the work. See U. Eco, *The Open Work* (trans. Anna Cancogni), Cambridge, MA: Harvard University Press, 1989.

12
Kusama's 'obsessional neuroses' continued throughout her time in New York. In 1964 her recurring illness became more frequent, she developed heart problems and was hospitalised on a number of occasions. In 1973 she returned to Tokyo. She was hospitalised at various times between 1975 and 1977, and since 1977 Kusama has voluntarily chosen to live at the Tokorozawa Seiwa Hospital, Kanto, Tokyo, Shinjuku district. See B. Karia (ed.), *Yayoi Kusama*, *op. cit.*, pp.97—100.

13
See, for example, Y. Kusama, 'The Struggle and Wanderings of My Soul' (1975), in L. Hoptman et al., *Yayoi Kusama*, *op. cit.*, p.119.

14
'Painting pictures has been therapy for me to overcome the illness.' Y. Kusama in conversation with Damien Hirst (1998), in L. Hoptman et al., *Yayoi Kusama*, *op. cit.*, p.136.

15
Y. Kusama, *Infinity Net*, *op. cit.*, p.20.

16
Ibid., p.69.

17
Ibid., p.20.

18
Briony Fer has discussed Roger Caillois's writing, including 'Mimicry and Legendary Psychasthenia' (1935), in relation to 1960s sculpture in 'Objects Beyond Objecthood', *Oxford Art Journal*, vol.22, no.2, 1999, pp.25—36.

19
See Charlotte Perkins Gilman, *The Yellow Wallpaper* (ed. Dale M. Bauer), Boston and New York: Bedford Books, 1998.

20
Ibid., p.43.

21
Ibid., p.57.

22
Ibid., p.58. Gilman's account, and Kusama's later descriptions of her own experiences of 'self-obliteration', share much with the female protagonist of Roman Polanski's 1965 horror film *Repulsion*, in which a young woman (played

by Catherine Deneuve) finds herself alone for a few days within the claustrophobic confines of her apartment, gradually succumbing to delusions and finally hysteria — murdering two men who visit her. By the film's end she experiences hands protruding from the walls, grabbing and stroking her body as she suffers fantasies of being attacked and sexually assaulted by a third male subject who appears to her at night.

23
Y. Kusama, 'The Struggle and Wanderings of My Soul', *op. cit.*, p.119.

24
See, for example, the press release for *Naked Event Outside the Stock Exchange*, New York, 14 July 1968, as quoted in B. Karia (ed.), *Yayoi Kusama*, *op. cit.*, p.91.

25
Y. Kusama, *Infinity Net*, *op. cit.*, p.42.

26
Ibid.

27
The recent 'participatory turn' in contemporary art and criticism has tended to privilege, over the private subjective encounter, the collective experience of the artwork in which audience members are brought together to eat, read or mingle. This approach — what, in another context, the French curator Nicolas Bourriaud dubbed 'relational aesthetics' — claims such work is inherently political in providing collective and participatory ventures. This position has been critiqued by writers including Hal Foster and Claire Bishop, who have pointed out that the mere fact of including the spectator within the artwork, event or happening is not automatically or necessarily a political gesture, and can quite often serve as one more instrument of spectacularisation. See N. Bourriaud, *Relational Aesthetics* (English Language Edition), Dijon: Les presses du réel, 1998; C. Bishop, 'Antagonism and Relational Aesthetics', *October*, vol.110, Fall 2004, pp.51—79; and H. Foster, 'Arty Party', *London Review of Books*, vol.25, no.23, 4 December 2003, reprinted in C. Bishop (ed.), *Participation*, London and Cambridge, MA: Whitechapel and The MIT Press, 2006, pp.190—95.

28
Helen Molesworth, 'Part Object Part Sculpture', in H. Molesworth (ed.), *Part Object Part Sculpture* (exh. cat.), University Park: Penn State Press, 2005, p.20.

29
Meret Oppenheim's *Object* is also known as *Le Déjeuner en fourrure* (*The Luncheon in Fur*), which was the title bestowed to the piece by André Breton.

30
Kusama used blood-red dip-dyed gloves again years later, in her series *End of Summer* (1980), *The Red Horizon* (1980) and *Sea of the Summer* (1983).

31
Quoted in Jan Cremer, 'On the Cover', *Art Voices*, Fall 1965, p.5. The short article was written to accompany the cover photograph of *My Flower Bed*, complete with Kusama curled up 'asleep'.

32
B. Fer, *The Infinite Line: Remaking Art after Modernism*, New Haven and London: Yale University Press, 2004, p.91.

33
See *Ibid.*, p.93.

34
'The first thing I did in New York was to climb up the Empire State Building and survey the city. I aspired to grab everything that went on in the city and become a star.' Y. Kusama in conversation with Akira Tatehata, in L. Hoptman et al., *Yayoi Kusama*, *op. cit.*, p.11.

35
In November 1955, Kusama wrote to Georgia O'Keefe to ask her advice on becoming an artist in the US. She was already beginning to achieve success in Japan for her surrealist watercolours, and she included several with the letter. O'Keefe responded kindly but honestly, pointing out how hard it would be to become established in the New York art world. Two years later, Kusama wrote again to let O'Keefe know she was coming to the US, to which O'Keefe responded, on 18 August, 'When you get to New York take your pictures under your arm and show them to anyone you think may be interested.' Quoted in B. Karia, *Yayoi Kusama*, *op. cit.*, pp.71—72.

36
See A. Munroe, 'Obsession, Fantasy and Outrage', *op. cit.*, p.30. In fact, in 1962, ostensibly Kusama's bona fide Pop art period, both she and Warhol produced very similar works comprising linear grids of airmail stamps. Warhol made *Red Airmail Stamps* using a rubber stamp to cover his 40 by 50-centimetre canvas, while for her much larger work *Air Mail Stickers*, Kusama glued actual airmail stamps directly onto the almost two-metre wide canvas.

37
In 1977 Kusama elected to move voluntarily into a psychiatric hospital in Tokyo, five minutes away from her studio. By the late 1980s, after several years of working predominantly on her writing, she had begun to regularly exhibit new work again, which included large-scale environmental installations similar to *Infinity Mirror Room — Phalli's Field*. *Dots Obsession* (1998), for example, a large mirrored room containing a series of big red inflatable balloons spotted with black polka dots, exists as a permanent installation at the Mattress Factory in Pittsburgh, Pennsylvania. Kusama also returned to making soft, stuffed sculpture alongside the large-scale polka dot and *Infinity Net* paintings, directly recalling her work of the 1960s.

38
Kusama has always hired professional photographers to document her exhibitions and performances, recognising the importance of preserving the event for her own personal archive as well as promotional use. One of these photographers, Rudolf Burckhardt, has recalled that Kusama was very involved with staging her shoots, and would frequently direct the photographer according to how she imagined it being 'used'. See M. Yoshimoto, *Into Performance*, *op. cit.*, p.63.

39
Mignon Nixon has written about the logic of the 'art object as part-object' in relation to the work of artists working in the 1950s and 60s, including Kusama: 'These parodies of the phallus (for parodies they are) had potential political effects: made literal, the phallus might be undermined as a patriarchal symbol. Indeed, rendered literal enough, it might be turned into an explicitly counter-patriarchal object, or rather part-object. For to parody the phallus by posing it was, in these and many other instances, also to propose it as a part-object.' M. Nixon, 'Posing the Phallus', *October*, vol.92, Spring 2000, p.99. Nixon also highlights the extent to which this recasting of the 'part-object' in postmodernist art practice was indebted to the 'complex historical reception' of Surrealism and Marcel Duchamp (p.104). Nixon includes Jasper Johns, Eva Hesse and Louise Bourgeois, along with Kusama, in this lineage.

40
A. Munroe, 'Obsession, Fantasy and Outrage', *op. cit.*, p.23.

41
See M. Nixon, 'Infinity Politics', in F. Morris (ed.), *Yayoi Kusama*, *op. cit.*, p.183.

42
Examples of those major recuperations of Kusama's work include 'Yayoi Kusama: A Retrospective' at the Centre for International Contemporary Arts, New York in 1989; 'Love Forever: Yayoi Kusama 1958—1968' at the Museum of Modern Art, New York and the Los Angeles County Museum of Art, Los Angeles in 1998; and 'Yayoi Kusama' at the Serpentine Gallery, London in 2000. In 1993 Kusama represented Japan for the 45th Venice Biennale. In 2000 Phaidon Press published a monograph on her work, as part of the 'Contemporary Artists' series. She was included in a number of important revisionist group exhibitions in the late 1980s and 90s, including 'L'Informe: Mode d'emploi' in 1996, curated by Yve-Alain Bois and Rosalind Krauss for the Centre Georges Pompidou, Paris, and 'Inside the Visible: An Elliptical Traverse of 20th Century Art in, of and from the Feminine' in 1996, curated by Catherine de Zegher for the Institute of Contemporary Arts, Boston and the Whitechapel Gallery, London. In 2011 'Yayoi Kusama', a major retrospective curated by Frances Morris, opened at the Museo Nacional Centro de Arte Reina Sofía, Madrid, before travelling to the Centre Georges Pompidou, Tate Modern, London and the Whitney Museum of American Art, New York.

43
For an example of Mieke Bal's argument about the 'theoretical object' (in relation to the work of Louise Bourgeois in particular), see M. Bal, 'Narrative Inside Out: Louise Bourgeois' Spider as Theoretical Object', *Oxford Art Journal*, vol.22, no.2, 1999, pp.103—26.

44
See Allan Kaprow, *Essays on the Blurring of Art and Life*, Berkeley and Los Angeles: University of California Press, 1993. Robert Rauschenberg's famous claim was that 'Painting relates to both art and life. Neither can be made. (I try to act in the gap between the two.)' R. Rauschenberg, untitled statement, in Dorothy C. Miller (ed.), *Sixteen Americans*, New York: Museum of Modern Art, 1959, p.58; reprinted in Kristine Stiles and Peter Selz (ed.), *Theories and Documents of Contemporary Art: A Sourcebook of Artists' Writings*, Berkeley and Los Angeles: University of California Press, p.321.

45
Y. Kusama, *Infinity Net*, *op. cit.*, p.151.

46
Kusama organised *The Anatomic Explosion, a series of Happenings*, staged between July and November 1968, in various locations in New York: in front of the statue of George Washington on Wall Street; at the foot of the Statue of Liberty; in St Mark's Church in-the-Bowery; at the *Alice in Wonderland* statue in Central Park; in front of the United Nations building, the United Federation of Teachers on Wall Street and the Board of Elections headquarters; and on the subway. The dates and locations suggest a close link to the 1968 US presidential election, a campaign that saw Richard Nixon elected and that was a wrenching national experience, conducted against a backdrop that included the assassination of Martin Luther King, Jr., subsequent race riots across the nation, the assassination of presidential candidate Robert F. Kennedy, widespread demonstrations against the Vietnam War across university and college campuses and violent confrontations between police and antiwar protesters at the 1968 Democratic National Convention.

47
The pig was probably referring to Pigasus the Immortal, the presidential candidate for the Youth International Party (Yippies), nominated by Abbie Hoffman and Jerry Rubin during the massive protest at the Democratic National Convention in Chicago in August 1968.

48
See Lewis Carroll, *Alice's Adventures in Wonderland*, Macmillan, London, 1865. See also L. Carroll, *Through the Looking-Glass, and What Alice Found There*, Macmillan, London, 1871. Kusama conflated the two books by Lewis Carroll.

49
See Y. Kusama, *Infinity Net*, *op. cit.*, p.42. The happening may have also been referencing the Boston Tea Party, which, since 1773 has been referenced in political protests by a variety of US activists (for example, one 'Tea Party' in 1973 invoked the impeachment of President Nixon).

50
Y. Kusama, *Infinity Net*, *op. cit.*, p.51.

51
See Midori Yamamura, 'Kusama and Nul: An International Crossroad of the Art of Social Engagement', in *Nul=0: The Dutch Group in an International Context* (exh. cat.), Schiedam: Stedelijk Museum and NAi Publishers, 2011, pp.84—88. See also L. Hoptman, 'Down to Zero: Yayoi Kusama and the European New Tendency', in Lynn Zelevansky et al., *Love Forever: Yayoi Kusama 1958—1968*, Los Angeles: Los Angeles County Museum of Art, 1998, pp.42—60. In 1966 the artist Lucas Samaras produced his own mirrored room, which, unlike Kusama's, is entirely constructed from mirrored square panels — the interior and exterior walls, floor, ceiling, door, table and chair — an uncompromisingly hard-edged room in which the viewer's body stands in stark contrast.

52
See C. Bishop, *Installation Art*, London: Tate Publishing, 2005, p.90; and Jacques Lacan, 'The Mirror Stage as Formative of the I Function as Revealed in Psychoanalytic Experience', *Écrits* (1966, trans. Bruce Fink), New York: W.W. Norton Company, 2002, pp.3—10.

53
Ibid., p.5.

54
Ibid.

55
See C. Bishop, *Installation Art*, *op. cit.*, p.92. The cover of Bishop's book shows a photograph of Kusama inside *Peep Show — Endless Love*.

56
Her work was already described as 'psychotic art' by Edward T. Kelly in 'Neo-Dada: A Critique of Pop Art', *Art Journal*, vol.23, no.3, Spring 1964, p.200.

57
See M. Nixon, 'Posing the Phallus', *op. cit.*; B. Fer, 'Objects Beyond Objecthood', *op. cit.*; and J. Mitchell, 'Portrait of the Artist as a Young Flower', *op. cit.*

58
M. Nixon, 'Posing the Phallus', *op. cit.*, p.114.

59
See Sigmund Freud, *The Complete Psychological Works of Sigmund Freud (The Standard Edition), Volume VII (1901—1905): A Case of Hysteria, Three Essays on Sexuality and Other Works, Volume I—VI* (ed. and trans. James Stracey), London: The Hogarth Press and the Institute of Psychoanalysis, 1953.

60
See D.W. Winnicott, 'Playing: A Theoretical Statement', *op. cit.*, pp.38—53.

61
See D.W. Winnicott, 'Creativity and its Origins', *Playing and Reality*, *op. cit.*, pp.65—86.

62
See Y. Kusama, *Infinity Net*, *op. cit.*, p.33. For a psychoanalytically informed account of the *Infinity Net* paintings, see Izumi Nakajima, 'Yayoi Kusama Between Abstraction and Pathology', in Griselda Pollock (ed.), *Psychoanalysis and the Image: Transdisciplinary Perspectives*, Oxford: Blackwell Publishing, 2006, pp.127—61.

63
See Donald Judd, 'Reviews and Previews: New Names This Month', *Art News*, October 1959; reprinted in D. Judd, *Donald Judd: The Complete Writings 1959—1975*, Halifax, Nova Scotia and New York: The Press of the Nova Scotia College of Art and Design, 1975, p.2.

64
On Niki de Saint-Phalle's *Tir* paintings, see Jill Carrick, 'Phallic Victories? Niki de Saint-Phalle's *Tirs*', *Art History*, vol.26, no.5, 2003, pp.700—29.

65
D. Judd, 'Reviews and Previews: New Names This Month', *op. cit.*, p.2.

66
Y. Kusama, *Infinity Net*, *op. cit.*, pp.23—26.

67
'Interview with Gordon Brown', first published in the book *De nieuwe stijl/The New Style: Werk van de internationale avant-garde*, vol.1, Amsterdam: De Bezige Bij, 1965, pp.163—64; reprinted in L. Hoptman et al., *Yayoi Kusama*, *op. cit.*, p.103.

68
D. Judd, *Donald Judd: The Complete Writings*, *op. cit.*, p.2.

69
For a discussion of the tableau format in the work of artists including Claes Oldenburg and Kusama, see B. Fer, 'Tableau', *The Infinite Line*, *op. cit.*, pp.85—101.

70
M. Nixon, 'Posing the Phallus', *op. cit.*, p.114.

71
Michael Fried, 'Art and Objecthood', *Artforum*, vol.5, no.10, June 1967, pp.12—23; reprinted in, among other collections, Gregory Battcock (ed.), *Minimal Art: A Critical Anthology*, Berkeley: University of California Press, 1995, pp.116—48.

72
Ibid., p.147.

73
Robert Morris's solo show at Richard Bellamy's Green Gallery became a defining moment in the history of Minimal art. The arrangement of the seven pieces in the gallery space and their relation to the room's geometry invited visitors to fully engage with the exhibiting space affecting circulation almost in a choreographic manner. The artworks, all referred to with the formula *Untitled (Object Name)*, and included, *Boiler*, *Cloud*, *Corner Beam*, *Corner Piece*, *Floor Beam*, *Table* and *Wall Slab*.

74
Robert Morris, 'Notes on Sculpture Part Two' (1966), *Artforum*, vol.5, no.2, October 1966, pp.20—23; reprinted in G. Battcock (ed.), *Minimal Art*, *op. cit.*, pp.233—34.

75
'Womanhouse' was a project realised by Judy Chicago and Miriam Shapiro in collaboration with the Feminist Art Program at California Institute of the Arts, Valencia, CA. During three months, between 1971 and 1972, the women students

renovated the dilapidated house at 553 Mariposa Avenue in Hollywood, Los Angeles and created installations, performances and works of art within it. 'Womanhouse' opened to the public from 30 January to 28 February 1972. For more information, see http://womanhouse.refugia.net and http://www.as-ap.org/content/womanhouse-cradle-feminist-art-sandra-sider-0 (last accessed on 31 May 2012).

76
On Kusama's relationship with her mother, see, for example, Y. Kusama, *Infinity Net*, *op. cit.*, pp.70—72.

77
For a discussion of Mona Hatoum's work and domesticity, see Tamar Garb, 'Hairlines', in C. de Zegher and Carol Amstrong (ed.), *Women Artists at the Millenium*, Cambridge, MA and London: The MIT Press, 2006, pp.255—75.

78
Kusama's '*Driving Image* Show' was installed in slightly different formats at the Richard Castellane's Gallery, New York in 1964, at Galleria del Naviglio, Milan in 1966 and at Galerie M.E. Thelen, Essen that same year. It involved a series of room-sized installations that included works from her *Sex-Obsession*, *Food-Obsession* and *Compulsion Furniture* series. While the *Sex-Obsession* works mainly comprised objects whose surfaces she would cover with white fabric bumps and protuberances, the *Food-Obsession* works consisted of a series of objects ranging from mannequins to suitcases covered in glued-on dried pasta. *Compulsion Furniture* includes the large armchair and sofa adorned with white phallic tubers.

79
Y. Kusama, artist's statement, 1964, as quoted in Udo Kultermann, '*Driving Image*, Essen, 1966', in L. Hoptman et al., *Yayoi Kusama*, *op. cit.*, p.89.

80
Y. Kusama, *Infinity Net*, *op. cit.*, p.47.

81
Ibid.

82
See U. Kultermann, '*Driving Image*, Essen, 1966', *op. cit.*, p.86.

83
D.W. Winnicott, 'Transitional Objects and Transitional Phenomena', *Playing and Reality*, *op. cit.*, p.5.

84
See Lucy R. Lippard, 'Eros Presumptive', *Hudson Review*, vol.20, no.1, Spring 1967, pp.91—99.

85
For this description, see M. Nixon, 'Posing the Phallus', *op. cit.*, p.118.

86
Amelia Jones, *Body Art/Performing the Subject*, Minneapolis: University of Minnesota Press, 1998, p.8.

87
This photograph is reproduced and discussed in Anna C. Chave, 'Striking Poses: The Absurdist Theatrics of Eva Hesse', in Geraldine Johnson (ed.), *Sculpture and Photography: Envisioning the Third Dimension*, Cambridge and New York: Cambridge University Press, 1998, p.171.

88
For a discussion of Lee Lozano's drawings, see J. Applin, 'Lozano's Labor', in Iris Muller-Westermann (ed.), *Lee Lozano* (exh. cat.), Stockholm: Moderna Museet, 2010; and H. Molesworth, 'Tune In, Turn On, Drop Out: The Rejection of Lee Lozano', *Art Journal*, vol.61, no.4, Winter 2002, pp.64—70.

89
The exhibition 'Eccentric Abstraction' took place from 10 September to 8 October 1966 at the Fischbach Gallery in New York. See also the related text L.R. Lippard, 'Eccentric Abstraction', *Art International*, vol.10, no.9, 20 November 1966, pp.28, 34—40.

90
See Rosalind Krauss, 'Allusion and Illusion in Donald Judd', *Artforum*, vol.4, no.9, May 1966, p.24; and B. Fer, 'Judd's Specific Objects', *On Abstract Art*, New Haven and London: Yale University Press, 2000, pp.131—53.

91
Y. Kusama, 'Press Release Naked Protest at Wall Street, New York, 10.30am, Sunday 15th October, 1968'.

92
Al Van Starrex, 'Naked Happenings', *Man*, October 1968, p.44.

93
The most famous exponents of the new cultural left's promotion of these ideals were Herbert Marcuse in his book *Eros and Civilisation* (1955) and Norman O. Brown in *Life After Death: The Psychoanalytical Meaning of History* (1959) and *Love's Body* (1966).

94
Quoted in B. Karia, *Yayoi Kusama*, *op. cit.*, p.30.

95
Y. Kusama, *Infinity Net*, *op. cit.*, pp.22 and 13.

96
Harold Rosenberg, 'The American Action Painters', *Art News*, vol.51, no.8, December 1952; reprinted in H. Rosenberg, *The Tradition of the New*, New York: Horizon Press, 1959, p.25.

97
Ibid.

98
See A. Kaprow, 'The Legacy of Jackson Pollock', *Art News*, vol.57, no.6, October 1958, pp.24—26 and 55—57; reprinted in A. Kaprow, *Essays on the Blurring of Art and Life*, *op. cit.*, pp.1—9.

99
Ibid., p.5.

100
J. Rodenbeck, *Radical Prototypes: Allan Kaprow and the Invention of Happenings*, Cambridge, MA and London: The MIT Press, 2011, p.29.

101
A. Kaprow, *Assemblage, Environments & Happenings*, New York: Harry Abrams, 1966, p.196.

102
Ibid., p.165.

103
Ibid., p.187.

104
Ibid. The photographs of Kusama appear on pages 26, 27 and 69.

105
The French art critic Michel Tapié first encountered their work in Japan and was an important mediator between the Japanese and the international art context in the 1950s.

106
From the outset the Gutai group worked with mail art and other kinds of printed matter in order to promote their work internationally. See Ming Tiampo, *Gutai: De-Centering Modernism Art*, Chicago: University of Chicago Press, 2011. For an account of the Japanese avant-garde in the 1950s and 60s, see also Shinichiro Osaki, 'Body and Place: Action in Postwar Art in Japan', in Paul Schimmel, Russel Ferguson and Kristine Stiles (ed.), *Out of Actions: Between Performance and the Object 1949—1979*, London: Thames & Hudson, 1998, pp.121—59. Kusama's 'grotesque penis-like' objects are briefly discussed on page 154.

107
Y. Kusama, *Infinity Net*, *op. cit.*, p.102.

108
Between November 2011 and March 2012 the Queensland Gallery of Modern Art held the exhibition 'Yayoi Kusama: Look Now, See Forever', over the course of which visitors were given brightly coloured round stickers to 'obliterate' a specially prepared white room, including all of its furniture and contents.

Another *Obliteration Room* was set up in February 2012 to accompany the Kusama retrospective exhibition at Tate Modern, London.

109
'Naked Self-Obliteration: Interview with Jud Yakult', in L. Hoptman et al., *Yayoi Kusama*, *op. cit.*, p.112.

110
For a reading of Kusama as a subject formed by a life lived under conditions of war, see M. Nixon, 'Infinity Politics', *op. cit.*, pp.176—85.

111
Ibid., p.185.

112
Félix Guattari, 'Les Riches Affects de Madame Yayoi Kusama', in *Yayoi Kusama: Infinity Explosion* (exh. cat.), Tokyo: Fuji Television Gallery, 1986; quoted in Y. Kusama, *Infinity Net*, *op. cit.*, p.17.

113
'Interview with Gordon Brown', in L. Hoptman et al., *Yayoi Kusama*, *op. cit.*, p.104.

114
Y. Kusama, 'The Struggle and Wanderings of My Soul', *op. cit.*, p.119.

115
Ibid.

116
Y. Kusama in conversation with Glenn Scott Wright, *Yayoi Kusama, London*, *op. cit.*

117
D. Judd, 'Reviews and Previews: New Names This Month', *op. cit.*, p.2.

118
Ibid.

119
U. Kultermann, '*Driving Image*, Essen, 1966', *op. cit.*, p.89.

120
'Take a Subway Ride from Jail to Paradise', press release for happening on the Carnasie Line MBT 14th SW, New York, Sunday noon, 17 November 1968; reprinted in L. Hoptman et al., *Yayoi Kusama*, *op. cit.*, p.114.

121
Hannah Arendt, 'Freedom and Politics: A Lecture', *Chicago Review*, vol.14, no.1, May 1960, p.28.

122
H. Arendt, *The Human Condition* (1958), Chicago: The University of Chicago Press, 1998, p.199.

123
Ibid.

124
Ibid., p.96.

125
She has described it as 'a form of collaboration without object ... without either a preconceived goal or a resulting product'. Johanna Drucker, 'Collaboration Without Object(s)', *Art Journal*, vol.52, no.4, 1993, pp.51—58.

126
Y. Kusama, *Infinity Net*, *op. cit.*, p.57.

127
See D. Judd, 'Specific Objects', *Arts Yearbook 8: Contemporary Sculpture*, New York: Arts Digest, 1965, pp.74—83.